You Can't Just Snap Out Of It: The Real Path to Recovery From Psychological Trauma:

Introducing the START NOW Program

Cover Design by Monica Zec
Book design by Microlucid Technology Pvt. Ltd.
Copy editing by Becky Kyle and Sheryl Dunn

Printed in the United States of America

While the authors have made every effort to provide accurate telephone numbers and Internet addresses at the time of publication, neither the publisher nor the authors assume any responsibility for errors or for changes that occur after publication. As well, the publisher does not have any control over and does not assume responsibility for authors' or third-party websites or their content.

Neither the publisher nor the authors are engaged in rendering professional advice or services to the individual reader. The ideas, procedures and suggestions contained in this book are not intended as a substitute for consulting with your physician. All matters regarding your health require medical supervision. Neither the authors or the publisher shall be liable or responsible for any loss or damage allegedly arising from suggestions or information in this book.

All of the above regarding publishers and authors also applies to Sheryl Dunn and Shelfstealer's Press who were associated with the development of this book. Most of the permissions were obtained by Sheryl Dunn and Shelfstealer's Press and were obtained exclusively for this book. See Appendix C for a list of permissions. Sheryl Dunn and Shelfstealers Press do not assume any liability for the contents of this book.

PRAISE FOR YOU CAN'T JUST SNAP OUT OF IT

Dr Bremner has written a must-have how-to guide to recovery from psychological trauma that is clear and easy to follow. This long awaited book from the eminent expert and researcher on traumatic stress is an excellent resource for self-recovery for trauma survivors.

--Robert Lemelson, PhD, adjunct professor of Anthropology at UCLA, and documentary filmmaker.

Dr. Bremner and Lai Reed have distilled their extensive, scholarly knowledge of trauma, its effects, and its treatment into a practical, usable, reader-friendly format. You Can't Snap Out of It should prove very helpful for survivors of all types of trauma, including combat. The book provides many strategies and exercises for coping trauma and for recovering from it.

--Colin A. Ross, M.D., author *Trauma Model Therapy*

ALSO by DR. J. DOUGLAS BREMNER

TRAUMA, MEMORY AND DISSOCIATION (Progress in Psychiatry, Edited with C. Marmar) American Psychiatric Press, 1998.

POSTTRAUMATIC STRESS DISORDER: A Comprehensive Text (Edited with P. Saigh). Allyn & Bacon, 1999.

BRAIN IMAGING HANDBOOK, W.W. Norton & Company, 2005.

DOES STRESS DAMAGE THE BRAIN? UNDERSTANDING TRAUMA-RELATED DISORDERS FROM A MIND-BODY PERSPECTIVE. W.W. Norton & Company, 2002.

BEFORE YOU TAKE THAT PILL: *Why the Drug Industry May Be Bad for Your Health: Risks and Side Effects You Won't Find on the Label of Commonly Prescribed Drugs, Vitamins, and Supplements,* Avery Trade, 2008.

THE GOOSE THAT LAID THE GOLDEN EGG: Accutane, the Truth that Had to be Told. Right Publishing, 2011., 2nd Edition from Laughing Cow Books, 2014.

THE FASTEST GROWING RELIGION ON EARTH: How Genealogy Captured the Brains and Imaginations of Americans. Laughing Cow Books, 2013.

A FRESH LOOK AT GREED. Laughing Cow Books, 2013.

More information about Dr. Bremner's books is at <u>dougbremner.com</u>

Table of Contents

LIST OF FIGURES

We dedicate this book to
Patty...and to Viola, Dylan, and Sabina.

INTRODUCTION

This book is a collaborative project between J. Douglas Bremner, M.D., and Lai Reed, M.B.A. It is a follow-up to the book *Does Stress Damage the Brain? Understanding Psychological Trauma from a Mind-Body Perspective,* published in 2002 by W.W. Norton & Company, Inc., for professional psychologists, psychiatrists, and social workers in the field of mental health and psychological trauma.

However, unlike that book, *You Can't Just Snap Out Of It* is for *you,* whether you are the person who is affected by psychological trauma, or you wish to help someone close to you.

We decided there were enough books that train people how to help you recover from psychological trauma, but there weren't enough books to help *you* in your recovery. We think you need your own book because we believe you must take charge of your own recovery.

That led to the development of the START-NOW program. START-NOW, which forms the last two chapters of this book, and is an easy way to remember the real path toward recovery from psychological trauma (not the gimmicky, or short-cut, fake paths that many will try to peddle to you). Each letter of START-NOW spells out words that remind you of your path toward recovery and healing from psychological trauma. When combined with the chapters "Tools for Coping with Stress" (Chapter 10) and "Better Lifestyles" (Chapter 11), it represents a useful collection of practical tools to help you in your recovery.

So here it is. *You Can't Just Snap Out Of It: The Real Path To Recovery from Psychological Trauma: Introducing the START-NOW Program.* We hope you like it, and find something useful for yourself or your friends and family. Keep on reading if you want tools to help you with your path toward recovery and healing.

Start Now!

CHAPTER 1: YOU CAN'T JUST SNAP OUT OF IT

This is a book about the psychology of trauma. As one of the experts in the field, I can tell you everything that happens to the brain when a person experiences a traumatic event, but it is only as a survivor that I can tell you what happens to the heart.

Although you might know something about my research on the effects of psychological trauma on the individual, you probably don't know about how psychological trauma has affected me personally. You see, to everyone around me, I am the picture of professional and personal success. To myself, however, I am still a five-year-old boy, reeling in shock at the sudden loss of his mother.

When Does Trauma Occur?

Trauma occurs when you experience a life-threatening event to yourself or someone close to you, accompanied by intense fear, horror or helplessness (as defined by the American Psychiatric Association). Trauma can leave an indelible imprint on the brain.

For example, if you look at the brain scans of some traumatized individuals, you can see shrinkage of brain regions — such as the hippocampus — that are involved in memory, or a failure in brain areas — like   the frontal cortex — that are supposed to turn off the fear response. What you can't see, but what is equally important, is what that trauma does to the survivor's self-image. How a person feels, how he perceives himself and the world can be dramatically altered after a traumatic experience.

Although trauma can wreak havoc on the brain and the psyche of individuals, as we will show in this book, **IT DOESN'T HAVE TO.** Whether trauma has these devastating effects or not depends on how we deal with it — or more precisely, how we don't deal with it.

One of the things that surprises me most is how poorly many professionals and lay people advise trauma victims. Despite the fact that we now have a large body of research literature on the disease, trauma victims are regularly told to do the opposite of what my research and the research of others shows to be effective. In a variety of ways, victims are told to "just get over it," to "put it behind them," to "snap out of it."

As my work demonstrates, you can't just "get over it" because trauma can change the parts of the brain involved in memory, which can then result in those traumatic memories playing over and over again. As a result of this change, you can't just stop the memories of your own free will.

However, although I know as a researcher that the brain can't just get over it, as a trauma survivor and a clinician, I know only too well the impulse to tell oneself and others to block it out, to move beyond it. There's something deeply human about the desire to not face the pain, to believe the old adage "out of sight, out of mind."

Trauma is a Disease

Unfortunately, it is this very notion—that we can and should block out traumatic memories—that serves in part to keep the brains of many people caught replaying the memory of the events in an endless cycle. In response to trauma, the heart and mind pull in opposite directions. While the brain endlessly repeats events, the heart is desperately telling the mind to move away, not to go there.

The problem with the idea that people should just get over it is that trauma is not a state of mind. It is not an attitude or a belief that needs to be changed. It is a disease, the "I can't stop thinking about it disease." You can't just forget about it, or will it away.

Could you will yourself out of diabetes? Or cancer? Of course not. So why would you be able to will yourself out of trauma? It's not any different.

Left alone, trauma won't heal itself. Trauma is like a virus. Just as a virus leads to disease, trauma can lead to a disease: trauma-related mental and physical symptoms.

If you mount an effective immune response to the virus, you won't get the disease. Some people have good immune systems; others have immune systems that don't go quite far enough, and in the end they get the disease. Others do not mount any immune response—they may get sick and even die.

Like a pathogen, trauma is a trigger that can lead to physical and mental disease if not recognized, dealt with, and addressed. Similar to the immune system's response to infection by a virus, we have mechanisms within us to deal with trauma...night soldiers waging a secret war, so secret we're not consciously aware of it. The immune response to trauma is something like that, although it is more mental and cognitive. If your immune system doesn't kick in to fight an infection, you need help. That's why we have antibiotics.

This book gives you a cognitive, or thinking, antibiotic for the treatment of trauma. It is about what happens when our desire to block out traumatic events is at war with a mind incapable of letting go of the memories.

Some trauma survivors will put on "a brave face," a false persona. On the outside, they are the picture of healthy, successful, mature adults, while on the inside they feel frozen in time, frozen in the grief and the pain of the event. This is a very common psychological response when the trauma is not adequately addressed at the time of the traumatic events. But this is just one possible reaction. People are extremely resourceful, and will look for all kinds of ways to suppress the memory of the traumatic events—from drinking or taking drugs, to working night and day, to having affairs.

Sometimes the attempt to suppress the trauma from their thoughts results in damage to the body in the form of heart disease or gastric ulcers. Occasionally, particularly when you are faced with a vivid reminder of the traumatic event, all attempts at suppression fail. This might cause the person to be thrown back to the events in what professionals call "a flashback."

The Key Moment for Me

My professional interest in psychological trauma crystallized the first time I was faced with a trauma victim who was in the midst of a flashback.

I was a psychiatry resident at Yale University Medical School. It was a humid night in August, and I was on overnight call duty at the Veterans Administration (VA) Hospital in West Haven, Connecticut.

I'd just managed to fall into a fitful sleep when the ring of the telephone pulled me back into the world of the living. The operator patched through a veteran who wanted to talk to the psychiatrist on call.

"Gotta get them out, gotta get them out," the voice on the other end of the line said.

"Excuse me, may I ask who is calling?"

"Gotta get them out, gotta get them out," he repeated in a robotic fashion.

"Who are you, where are you calling from?"

"Gotta get them out. Gotta get them out."

"In order for me to help you, you've got to tell me who you are and what happened tonight."

"Gotta get them out. Gotta get them out."

This went on for twenty minutes. After a while, I talked him down and found out what was going on.

Earlier that night, the veteran rushed into a burning house to rescue three little children. He saved their lives. He was a hero.

But his mind paid a terrible price.

In the Vietnam War, he'd served as a fireman. His job was to put out fires on helicopters hit by enemy fires, including removing people from the flaming aircraft. Sometimes this meant saving lives; other times, it involved just pulling charred bodies out of the wreckage.

His actions as the hero who pulled the three children safely out of the house triggered a flashback to his memories of Vietnam. All he could see, like a movie playing out before him over and over, was a memory from Vietnam, rushing into a burning helicopter and pulling out the charred remains of a twenty-two-year-old marine.

As a last resort, he called the psychiatrist on duty at the VA hospital. Even as he talked to me on the phone, he replayed over and over, like a skip on a vinyl record, or like a continuous computer loop, pulling that body out of the helicopter.

When he came back into the land of the living, and while he was telling me his story, I had an epiphany: I realized that this man strongly resembled someone in the throes of a seizure, similar to my patients with brain disorders such as epilepsy. Even though they might look as though they're performing recognizable behaviors, epileptic patients in the midst of a seizure are in fact totally out of touch with the world around them.

It was at that moment that I first considered the possibility that an emotional event such as a trauma could cause real physiological damage to the brain.

(People use the word 'flashback' fairly loosely, but as it applies to Post Traumatic Stress Disorder (PTSD), it refers to a specific symptom, where you see a traumatic event from your past playing out like a movie in front of your eyes, and you

have no control over it. When people have a flashback, they are temporarily out of touch with what is going on around them.)

Changing Views on Trauma

While today that thought might not seem heretical, in the late 80's, such an idea would have been laughed at.

The prevailing 80's notion with psychological trauma cases was that the victims were malingerers, even though the American Psychiatric Association (APA)'s *Diagnostic and Statistical Manual* (DSM), the bible of psychiatry, described its diagnosis as Post-traumatic Stress Disorder, or PTSD. That diagnosis was virtually never used. It wasn't used because, frankly, I and almost all other professionals didn't believe in it.

Doctors are not islands; they reflect the beliefs and attitudes of their culture, time and place. When society changes, so do they.

At that time, "Just snap out of it, just get over it" was akin to a national theme song. We looked to the resilient super-survivors, the WWII veterans from the "Greatest Generation," who were (supposedly) unscarred by their war-time experiences, and who showed great courage and sacrifice for the country. We saw them as the ideal model — the ideal model being the person who could endure traumatic experiences and come out unscathed.

The thought that trauma might actually affect an individual — be that individual a soldier, a rape victim, or any other trauma survivor — was anathema to us.

Even today, many mental health professionals are still singing the "Just get over it" theme song. It resonates with the pull-yourself-up-by-the-bootstraps American outlook on life. For example, in a best-selling book *Cope With It!*, at page 147 of that book, the popular radio psychologist Dr. Laura Schlessinger writes,

> *Do you hold onto the past? Do you find yourself constantly reiterating old hurts? Might it be that remembering old pain serves a new purpose? Your old pain might be the way you manipulate your present partners or friends . . It also*

might be the way you get yourself off the hook for not being more giving, less selfish.

By saying this, Dr. Laura suggests that people with traumatic pasts are not only malingerers who should "just get over it" or "just snap out of it" (as she has said so many times on the radio), but that they are also manipulators. She implies that people hang onto the trauma to use as a weapon against others.

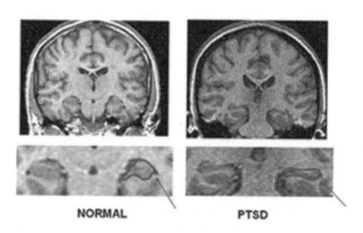

NORMAL   **PTSD**

FIGURE 1 HIPPOCAMPAL VOLUME IN PTSD

Measured with magnetic resonance imaging (MRI). There is a visible reduction in volume of the hippocampus (outlined in red) in a representative patient with PTSD relative to a normal individual (arrow). Used by permission..

That was (and in some quarters still is) the attitude towards trauma and its victims, but with that one Vietnam veteran's case, I began to consider that perhaps we were wrong about psychological trauma. I wanted to discover the answers.

The Beginning of My Research

I started a research program at Yale where I used a magnetic resonance imaging (MRI) scanner to look at the brains of trauma victims.

The results astounded me.

The part of the brain involved in learning and memory called the hippocampus was smaller in trauma victims with PTSD. Studies in animals were showing that stress hormones actually caused shrinkage of neurons in the hippocampus. Now I had definite proof that many trauma victims were suffering from a real physiological disease — a disease that made it virtually impossible to "just get over it" after a trauma.

What I didn't know then was how to cure it. The answer to that question came only after many more years of research, clinical work, and much soul searching about my own life.

This book is the fruit of that work. Drawing on my lab work, my own story and a host of clinical cases, I explain what a psychological trauma is, what happens to the individual as a result of that trauma, and the process of recovery.

My co-worker Lai Reed and I outline the path to recovery, with our START-NOW program, the letters of the acronym spelling out how one can learn to really and finally "get over it." Together with Chapter 10 (Tools for Coping with Stress), we've provided a road map toward personal psychological recovery and healing. We also include useful information for the loved ones of trauma victims, since they can be an invaluable part of the recovery process, as well as additional resources at the end of this book.

So let's get our engines started.

Happy motoring!

CHAPTER 2: HIDDEN WOUNDS

When I was four years old, my father, a psychiatrist, took me to the office on a Saturday because he had to see a patient. I sat on the floor outside his office wondering what sort of magic he was performing in there. I knew he could cure people just by talking with them which, to my four-year-old mind, made him a verbal magician.

Later that year, my mother died of meningitis, a bacterial infection of the brain. She was happy and healthy one day, and gone the next. I was filled with pain and grief. The person to talk to about my feelings was, of course, my father. Who better than the man whose magic words healed many?

Why Trauma Makes Us Lose Our Voice

For reasons I did not understand at the time, my father did not talk to me about how I felt. Most days he came home at six o'clock and just sat in a large leather chair in the living room drinking his scotch and reading his newspaper.

I was in enormous pain, but I was told, either directly or indirectly, that I should "get on with life" and "get over it," "grow up." My father remarried within the year, and did his best to get on with his own life.

All photographs and reminders of our mother were removed from sight. We were told by our parents that our biological mother was "messy" and a bad discipliner of her children. The implication was that we were better off without her.

You would think that my father would have known better, but even he, a trained psychiatrist, did not know how to deal with the trauma of my mother's death. He tried to blot it out of his mind, to not talk about it. As a professional, he knew that was the wrong thing to do, but as a grieving husband and father, he couldn't face the pain.

For that, he, together with my siblings and I, would later pay the price.

The Heavy Cost of Losing Your Mother

After my mother's death, I became a chronic bed-wetter, and lost about ten IQ points in my ability to perform in school. My mother's death became an open wound that did not heal.

Whenever someone asked me about my mother and I told them she had died, I felt as if the scab had been ripped off and made to start bleeding afresh. I was plagued by chronic self-doubt and low self-esteem.

I felt bad about myself, so I wanted reassurance from other people that I wasn't really so terrible after all. I felt that if people could see me for what I was, they would be revolted. I incorporated the pain, grief, and ugliness of what happened to my mother into my life and into my concept of myself.

The way in which one deals with trauma soon after the event is critical in determining whether a person will recover or go on to develop long-term problems. Since research shows that three out of four Americans will be traumatized at some time in their lives, it is important that everyone — both professionals and lay people — have an understanding of appropriate first steps. But first, I'll need to explain what constitutes a psychological trauma.

Psychological Trauma Defined

Psychological trauma (as defined by the American Psychiatric Association) is a threat to the life of yourself or someone close to you, accompanied by intense fear, horror, or helplessness. Traumatic events include childhood physical or sexual abuse, accidents, natural disasters, assault, rape, warfare or losing a parent or a child.

In about one out of five people, trauma can lead to chronic psychiatric symptoms, like post-traumatic stress disorder (PTSD), depression, or alcohol or substance abuse. Eight percent of Americans (or about 30 million people) get PTSD at some time in their lives, and 15% get depression (often triggered by traumatic events). Both disorders are twice as common in women as in men. The most common cause of PTSD in women is childhood sexual abuse, and in men it is physical assault. In about half of people, PTSD will eventually go away.

How Do We Respond to Psychological Trauma?

Many people exposed to a single traumatic event will do fine in the long run. For a limited time, they may suffer nightmares, or feel momentarily worse when something reminds them of the traumatic event, but if they have friends and family they can talk to, and who will listen and provide support, they will come out OK.

Some may benefit from short-term counseling. Others are just naturally resilient. For them, no matter what happens, they survive. Maybe what they need to do to recover just comes naturally to them.

However, not everyone is so lucky. Unfortunately, an all too common initial response is to try and block out the memory of the event, as occurred in my family. In Chapter 4 will discuss how such a response makes it impossible to really recover from the trauma.

Other times people can't recover because they are hit with several traumatic events one right after the other, BLAM, BLAM, BLAM! They don't have time to deal with them all.

You might be able to get over one trauma without too much effort . . . maybe. But in my experience, when the traumas keep coming, one after the other, sooner or later you get stuck. And then, no matter how many times you tell yourself to get over it, or other people say the same thing, it doesn't happen. Not on its own, at least.

Let's take a closer look at how and why this happens.

Trauma Reverberates

Sometimes people experience something bad... and then it gets worse. It's like the old saying, "Out of the frying pan and into the fire."

Say you're in a hurricane. First, you are exposed to the trauma of the hurricane itself; then you have to deal with losing friends and relatives; possibly you lose your house, your community is destroyed, you lose your job, have to move because you can't afford the rent, your children are uprooted from their schools, etc., etc. See how it works?

What if you develop symptoms of PTSD or depression? You think you had it bad before. Now it only gets worse.

It's easy to see how the trauma can quickly become a chronic event. Living in a situation where you are constantly re-exposed to additional traumas makes it impossible to adequately process the earlier ones, leading to increased problems.

Get In Line to Grieve

One of my patients told me he couldn't grieve for his father who'd just died, because he had five or six other deaths he hadn't dealt with yet. His father had to "take a number."

There are other reasons why people have trouble getting over trauma. People who are younger or less educated in general do worse after a trauma, perhaps because they don't have the mental tools or experience to work through the event in their minds. Also, when people don't have someone to talk to, or they get unhelpful advice, like "put it behind you" or "just snap out of it" or "just get over it", research studies show they do worse.

These groups develop psychological problems such as PTSD and depression, and it is these people whose brains are changed, sometimes forever, by trauma. Granted, some people may get all the support they need, and still develop psychological problems. What is common to all people who develop problems after exposure to psychological trauma are changes in the brain, something we will talk about in the next chapter.

CHAPTER 3: EFFECTS OF TRAUMATIC STRESS ON THE BRAIN

One reason why it can be difficult to just get over psychological trauma on your own is that trauma can have effects on the brain. As discussed in the book *Does Stress Damage the Brain? Understanding Trauma-related Disorders from a Mind-Brain Perspective*, changes in the brain after trauma can affect the behavior and emotions of the trauma victim. And it can do this in a way that makes it basically impossible to simply "will" yourself out of the situation.

To understand how psychological trauma affects the brain, we must first understand something about the nature of the brain itself.

Our Mysterious Brains

The brain is the most complicated, but also the most interesting, organ of the body. It is the central clearinghouse of everything that matters to us as individuals.

Prior civilizations considered the heart or the liver to be the center of the personal essence or spirit. The Greeks had a word called "thumos," meaning courage or strength of character. They thought thumos was in the chest somewhere.

People still use phrases like "he has a good heart" or they talk about someone "dying of a broken heart." Some of those old ideas about emotions living in the chest haven't completely gone away.

Today we would put thumos in the brain, and think of it as related to the mind. Now we know that the mind is in the brain. That is why there has been a sudden burst of interest in the field of neuroscience amongst the general public.

People want to learn more about themselves and how they fit into the world. Many people now realize that the brain, rather than being something relegated to dry textbooks, is a thing of mystery and complexity. It is important to understand and celebrate it, something to be embraced as a rich source of knowledge that will help us on our path toward a greater understanding of ourselves.

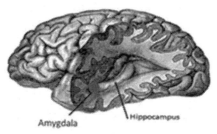

FIGURE 2: DIAGRAM OF THE HUMAN BRAIN SHOWING THE HIPPOCAMPUS AND AMYGDALA

Diagram of the human brain from the side with a cut-away section showing the hippocampus (colored in blue) and amygdala (colored in red). The frontal lobe (front of the brain) is on the left side of the diagram. The amygdala sits at the head of the hippocampus. There is a hippocampus and amygdala on both the left and the right sides of the brain. (Source: Wikipedia)

Understanding the Brain as Part of the Process of Recovery

For you, on the road to recovery from psychological trauma, getting to know your brain is a critical part of the process of recovery from psychological trauma. That is why it is good news that you have brain experts to help you on your road to recovery.

How do things in the world affect us? How do we taste, hear and feel, and how can these things influence our emotions, our sense of self and others?

Studies showed that previously healthy journalists who watched executions of prisoners were often affected for years afterward by mental health problems, even though they didn't personally know the person being executed, even though they were not physically harmed or injured in any way (at least on the outside.) Why is it that passively watching something like an execution can have such a devastating impact on us? Why is it that the witnessing of a terrible event, acting through our vision, hearing, smell, and other senses, can change our lives, possibly forever?

To answer these questions, we have to learn a little bit about how the brain and the physical senses work.

How the Brain Perceives the World

Then we smell something, small amounts of substances are emitted from the thing we smell that physically enter our nose and travel through little holes in the top of our nose, in an area called the cribriform plate. They next land on a part of the brain, the olfactory cortex, that is responsible for smell.

Isn't that amazing?

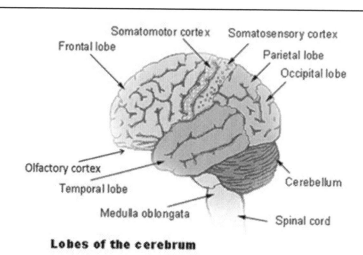

Lobes of the cerebrum

FIGURE 3: VIEW OF THE SURFACE OF THE HUMAN BRAIN

The cerebrum, or cerebral cortex, is at the outer part of the brain, and includes frontal and temporal lobes and other areas. The frontal lobe is involved in thought and emotion and suppression of fear reactions from the amygdala. The olfactory cortex, that processes smell, is in the orbitofrontal cortex at the bottom part of the frontal lobe. The somatomotor cortex controls movement of the body. The somatosensory cortex processes feelings of touch. The visual cortex that processes what we see is in the occipital lobe, which is at the back of the brain. Auditory cortex (sound) is in the temporal lobe. The brain stem, which controls basic processes like breathing or sleep, is the pink area, and includes medulla oblongata and spinal cord. (Source: Wikipedia)

This brain area sends the information on to the rest of the brain. For instance, if you smell rotting meat, invisible pieces of the meat waft in the air (because they are so small they can get blown around easily), travel through your nose, and are detected by the brain as having something wrong with them.

The olfactory cortex then sends a signal to the fear area of the brain, called the *amygdala*, that says, "Danger, danger! We've got rotten meat here that may contain bacteria and kill you if you eat it. I don't care how hungry you are, don't do it! There likely will be a mastodon to come along soon and you can kill that one and eat it."

The amygdala sounds the alarm, causing hormones like cortisol and norepinephrine to flood the body. This results in increases in heart rate and blood pressure and breathing, as well as shifts in where body energy is sent to in the body, that may help us survive.

We'll talk in more detail   e body during the fear response.

Different parts of the brain work together to process what's going on in the world. They have to work together as an effective team. If they didn't, we wouldn't survive.

Everything we see, smell, hear, taste and touch gets processed by different parts of the brain. If the brain detects a threat, it activates the fear response. If you walk down a path in the jungle and bump into a lion, a series of things happen in your brain that end up with the thought, "Get the heck out of here!"

The vision of the lion comes in through the eyes and is sent to a part of the brain called the primary visual cortex, or occipital lobe, which is in the very back of the brain. It then goes to the secondary visual association cortex, right next to it, where a more complicated processing of the vision takes place. The lion growls, and the noise comes in through the ears and is sent to the auditory cortex, a part of the brain in the temporal lobe that processes sounds.

The parts of the brain involved in memory, the hippocampus and frontal cortex, pull this information together and compare it to prior experiences of running into a lion. If there's a match, the information is sent to the amygdala, which cranks up your heart rate, blood pressure, and breathing. You brain then tells you "Let's get out of here!" Otherwise, you might become lunch.

The Science of Fear Learning

Specific parts of the brain are involved in learning fear. In experiments with rats where you pair a bright light with a shock, exposure to the light alone will cause a fear reaction. This is called fear acquisition, fear conditioning, or acquisition of conditioned fear. It is called conditioning, because we become "conditioned," or learn to be afraid, in specific situations.

If there is damage to the amygdala, animals don't learn fear reactions. That tells us that we learn fear, or acquire conditioned fear responses, with the amygdala.

The ability to learn fear reactions is very important for survival, absolutely necessary, in fact. If we don't learn fear, we become somebody else's lunch.

PTSD is the Failure to Unlearn Fear

Just as important as learning fear, is the ability to unlearn it. Although not learning fear will make you into lunch, not being able to unlearn it will make you miserable — you might wish you had been lunch.

To get back to our rats, with continued exposure to the light without the shock, the animal will "learn" there is no danger associated with the light, and the fear reaction will go away. This is called "extinction" of fear. It results from the frontal cortex (the part of the brain in the front) sending signals to turn off the amygdala. Animals with damage to the frontal cortex have problems turning off the fear response. PTSD is like a kind of failure to unlearn fear.

A guy named Phineas Gage, who lived about 100 years ago, had a railroad spike go into his frontal cortex and damage that part of the brain. After that, although he had normal speech and seemed OK, he had difficulties regulating his emotions and interacting with other people. This led doctors to the idea that this part of the brain was involved in emotion.

Did you ever get in a car accident? Remember how right after that you were afraid to get behind the wheel again? And that after a while when you kept driving, because otherwise how else would you get to work, the fear reaction went away? That is an example of fear acquisition and extinction. People with PTSD are not able to turn off the fear reaction normally, which is what often makes them disabled.

Sometimes It's Better Not to Go on Vacation

Sigmund Freud, the great Austrian psychoanalyst, said that you have to go on vacation for at least a month to get any benefit out of it. People do that in Europe, where my wife comes from. In fact, everyone goes to the beach for the entire month of August. Although we don't do that in the U.S., everyone agrees that vacation is a good thing.

Actually that isn't always true. I'll tell you why in a minute.

One of the things I love about giving lectures to a new groups of people is that, while I have something to teach them about my knowledge and expertise in psychiatry and neuroscience, they usually have equally useful and information for me. For example, many years ago I gave a lecture about psychological trauma to a group of Navy psychiatrists in Norfolk, Virginia. After the lecture, the psychiatrists talked about some of their patients who were on active duty.

One of the psychiatrists shared a story of an enlisted man in the Navy who was on a submarine that experienced an on-board explosion while out to sea. No one was injured, but the Navy thought they would do him a favor and give him a week of shore leave. It turned out not to be a favor at all.

When he walked out on the dock at the end of his leave time to get back on the sub, he couldn't make himself move. By keeping him away from the source of the accident, they hadn't allowed his normal fear extinction functions to work. His fear became ingrained in his brain, and now it would be harder than ever to get over it. You see, it would have been better if they didn't give him a vacation. I'm not sure if that sailor ever did get back on a submarine.

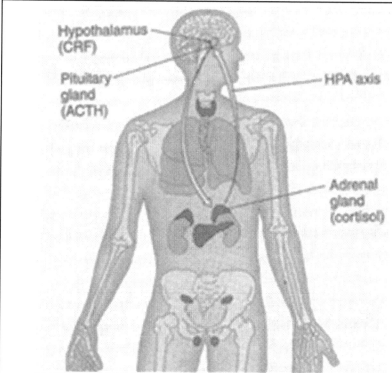

FIGURE 4: NEUROHORMONAL RESPONSES TO STRESS

Each of the body glands produces and releases hormones into the blood-stream. The arrow shows the hypothalamic-pituitary-adrenal (HPA) axis, which controls release of the stress hormone, cortisol. Used with permission.

Stress Hormones and the Fear Response in Survival

Part of team brain response to survival is an outpouring of stress hormones like norepinephrine and cortisol that flood the body during stress. Like the amygdala, they also help us survive. Let's see how they work.

A collection of brain cells (or neurons) in the brain stem (the part of the brain at the back of your neck that controls basic functions like breathing and being awake) contains the majority of the stress hormone, adrenaline, in the brain. Technically, it is known as noradrenaline (norepinephrine) when it occurs in the brain and adrenaline (epinephrine) in the body, but I refer to both using the commonly known term "adrenaline."

These brain cells have long fibers, known as axons, that extend their tentacles throughout the brain, and release adrenaline everywhere all at once. This release is triggered by a scary event, like the attack of a lion. Adrenaline acts like a chemical messenger that says "RUN!!"

Adrenaline is the Brain's Fire Alarm System

When there's a fire, you run and pull an alarm that tells everyone in the building to get out right away. The idea is to tell everyone to leave, both the people who might get burned and those who are not at risk. There will be time to sort that out later, but in the short term it is better to make sure that everyone is safe.

Our brains and bodies have their own fire alarm system. It's called adrenaline. When there's a threat, adrenaline is released everywhere, signals all parts of the brain to pay attention, and triggers all parts of the body to be ready. Adrenaline makes blood pressure go up and heart rate increase so that you can deliver more blood to your brain, muscles, and the other parts of the body important to survival. You breathe faster so you get more oxygen into your lungs and then your blood. More blood means more oxygen and more energy (sugar) to help those body parts work better, so you can run faster and fight harder.

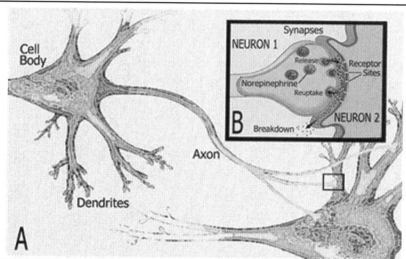

FIGURE 5: THE NEURON: BASIC CELL OF THE HUMAN BRAIN

The neuron

(a) has a long axon, at the end of which neurotransmitters are released into the space between the cells, called the synapse

(b) neurotransmitters travel through the synapse, where they attach to an adjacent neuron's dendrites, which are branching ends of the neuron that receive signals from adjacent neurons. Reuptake sites (where SSRI medications such as Prozac work) "vacuum" the neurotransmitter back into the neuron.

Cortisol Chips In

At the same time that your adrenaline system is firing, corticotropin releasing factor (CRF) is released from a part of the brain called the hypothalamus. This triggers a chain reaction which results in the release of the stress hormone, cortisol, from the adrenal gland.

Cortisol helps to move energy to the muscles so we can fight back or run away fast. It does this by moving energy away from areas that aren't needed for survival, like the stomach (you don't need to digest your lunch right away) or reproductive organs. Fast thinking and strong muscles are critical to survive at that split second when we are under attack.

Too Much of a Good Thing

We need the hormones cortisol and adrenaline to help us survive, but if we are under stress for too long, or there are too many traumatic events, they can get out of whack.

In some cases, CRF and adrenaline can be chronically too high; as well, minor stressors or things that trigger memories of stress may cause you to release way too much cortisol and norepinephrine. The cortisol system may get burnt out, it might not have the right rhythm, or it might be depleted at certain times of the day.

The fear part of the brain, the amygdala, may be over-active, and the parts of the brain involved in memory and emotion and turning off the fear response (the hippocampus and frontal cortex) may not turn on normally. You might use alcohol and drugs to turn off these stress hormones and quiet your brain so that you don't feel so anxious, but that can become a problem in itself. We will talk more about brain areas involved in stress later on.

How Psychological Trauma Affects the Brain: Case Study

I once had a patient who was a successful executive in a manufacturing company who had to travel frequently for business.

One morning, she was staying at a hotel and opened the door to see if the newspaper was there. A homeless man lurked in the hallway eating food off of the trays left out the night before. He pushed his way into her room and assaulted her. He had been drinking coffee off the trays in the hallway so he had coffee on his breath. He pulled on her hair from behind while he attempted to sodomize her. She managed to get away and alert hotel security, who had him arrested.

Following this, her body's fear response system activated when things reminded her of the event, even when no true threat existed. The smell of coffee caused an outpouring of adrenaline in her body, just as it did when she was assaulted. Her heart rate and blood pressure went up, and she started breathing rapidly.

When her three-year-old daughter pulled on her hair while playing, it made her feel extremely anxious and fearful. Her heart raced, and she felt as though she had to get away. This made it difficult for her to spend time with her daughter. She developed other symptoms of PTSD, like being jumpy and easily startled, having nightmares and flashbacks of the event, having trouble sleeping and concentrating, and trying to avoid things that reminded her of the event.

Whereas before she had a job with a lot of responsibility, she now found it difficult to get through the day. She had problems remembering things.

She said, "Lately I feel like my mind is degenerating, like I have some horrible dementing illness, I can't remember anything or think about anything normally. I walk into a room and I see something I've never seen before, and I say to myself, 'I've never seen that before, where did that come from?' I feel like I am falling apart."

When we read back a description of her rape incident to her in the laboratory while measuring her stress hormones, her body flooded with the stress hormone, cortisol, three or four times higher than normal, and her heart rate and blood pressure increased dramatically. We next read a description of the trauma to her while she was lying in a positron emission tomography (PET) camera, which measures brain function. The part of the brain responsible for thinking clearly and putting a brake on anxiety reactions, called the frontal cortex, shut down, as did her hippocampus, a brain area involved in memory. Other brain areas that drive the fear response were put in overdrive.

The Brain Remembers Trauma

Memories for the things that happen to us in daily life are formed by a brain area called the hippocampus, but the hippocampus doesn't store everything in memory forever. Sherlock Holmes's sidekick, Dr. Watson, had a theory about memory he called the Crowded Lumber Room Theory that was actually correct. It you put some wood into a crowded lumber room, you're going to have to take some other wood out to make room for the new wood. It is the same for memory. Store some new memories, take other ones out.

How does the brain do this? It stores the memories for a short time in the hippocampus. After the course of hours or days, some memories get moved into long-term storage in the cerebral cortex. This process is called *memory consolidation.*

But how does the brain decide which memories should be kept and which discarded? Obviously some memories are more important to keep than others. A lion attack is an experience you will probably never forget. That's a good thing, because the next time you see a lion, you be prepared to take appropriate action.

How does your brain keep the memory of the lion and not the memory of what you had for breakfast this morning? When cortisol and adrenaline are released during stress, they act on brain areas like the hippocampus that are involved memory to strengthen the memory trace. These hormones also tie the memory to the actual memories of the emotion, stored in a brain area called the amygdala. That way, the next time you see the lion, your fear response will come back right away, which will then prepare your body to deal with the potential threat.

Effects of Trauma on the Brain

The brain doesn't always respond to trauma in the most efficient way. The flood of stress hormones can cause damage to the hippocampus, the brain area responsible for forming memories. The stress hormones can also make the memory fragmented, dream-like, or distorted in other ways.

Depending on their concentration and how your brain has been affected by psychological trauma, stress hormones may cause you not to remember some things or some parts of your trauma well or not at all. In some cases, the hormonal response to stress is permanently changed, so that whenever you have a reminder of the event (like seeing a lion again), cortisol and adrenaline flood into the brain.

The flooding of these hormones also affects how the memory is recalled. The memory can pop into your mind at all times of the day and night, *so that you can't stop thinking about it* – like when you try to save a document on a computer in the midst of crashing. The document is often stored in a damaged way. As a result, every time you go to turn on the computer, the document pops up onto the screen. *It doesn't wait until you decide to access it.*

Monkey See, Monkey Don't Remember

When I started out as a researcher in psychiatry, working in an inpatient hospital unit for the treatment of Vietnam veterans with PTSD, we saw a presentation by a famous neuroscientist named Robert Sapolsky, PhD, about the effects of stress on the brain of monkeys.

He found that male monkeys who had been severely stressed by being caged with female monkeys (the females beat up the males in that particular species of monkey) had damage to the part of the brain involved in learning and memory called the hippocampus.

The brain cells, or neurons, showed a loss of the normal branching that under a microscope looks like the branches of a tree – the stressed monkeys had hippocampal neurons that looked like a withered tree.

Other scientists later found that the hippocampus was unique in the brain, the area where new neurons could be developed in adulthood. Stress unfortunately had the effect of turning off the growth of new neurons.

Smaller Hippocampal Volume in PTSD Patients

We wondered if stress could have a similar effect in our combat veterans, so we used magnetic resonance imaging (MRI) to measure the size of this brain structure in our veterans with PTSD. To our surprise, we found an 8% reduction in volume in this brain area. Later studies showed that people with PTSD from childhood abuse also had a reduction in volume in this area.

When we gave tests of the kind of memory the hippocampus is responsible for—learning new things like what to buy at the grocery store, or remembering the content of a story that was read out loud—they showed significant impairments. Since then many other research groups and scientists have had similar findings in a range of different groups of patients with PTSD.

For instance, when we did an MRI scan of the brain of the woman who had been a rape victim in a hotel that I described above, and measured the size of her hippocampus, we found it to be reduced in size, consistent with a stress-induced shrinkage.

PTSD as a Memory Disorder

We like to think of PTSD as a memory disorder because many PTSD patients have trouble remembering things, like where they have to go or what they have to do that day, while other things, especially their trauma, they can't get out of their minds. That is why we call it the "can't stop thinking about it disease."

While some parts of the trauma come back as repetitive intrusive memories, other important details of the trauma can't be remembered at all. One of the possible consequences of psychological trauma are symptoms of dissociation. These include feelings of being unreal, out of body, gaps in memory, or feeling like you are in a dream or a daze.

Trauma victims with the most severe hippocampal shrinkage have the most trouble with memory and the most dissociative symptoms. These victims have the greatest trouble because the hippocampus is responsible for memory as well as our perception of where we are in time and space (felt to represent a critical aspect of dissociation). We talk about dissociation in more detail later.

The Frontal Cortex Saves the Day (Or Not)

Another brain area that plays an important role in controlling our anxiety and fear reactions is the frontal cortex. This brain area has grown and grown as humans have evolved and is what makes us different from monkeys and all other animals down the line. The growth of this part of the brain allowed us to do all sorts of awesome things like make things, talk to each other, write books like this one, and figure out in our heads whether we have enough money to buy a latte at Starbuck's.

Unfortunately, getting a bigger brain also had its drawbacks. It's because we have this humongous brain area that we spend way too much time worrying about things we don't have any control over, anyway. This part of the brain is also sensitive to stress. Animals exposed to stress early in life have a decrease in branching of the neurons in this part of the brain. If there is something that looks like it might be scary, but isn't really, this brain area shuts off the fear reaction from the amygdala. We found that patients with PTSD, whether it is from childhood trauma or combat trauma, don't activate this part of the brain normally when they are listening to a script of their childhood trauma or watching combat scenes. We think this brain problem is the reason they have fear reactions all the time, even if there isn't something that is a real danger to them.

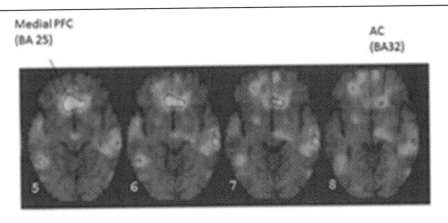

FIGURE 6: EFFECTS OF TRAUMATIC REMINDERS ON BRAIN FUNCTION

Brain activation with exposure to traumatic reminders measured with positron emission tomography (PET) brain imaging. The image shows where there are difference in blood flow in the brain between combat veterans with and without PTSD while viewing combat-related slides and sounds. Combat veterans withà PTSD compared to those without PTSD had a decrease in brain function in the medial prefrontal cortex (PFC) (yellow area), including the anterior cingulate (AC), during exposure to combat-related slides and sounds. Used by permission from J. Douglas Bremner, M.D.

The Stress Response Gone Haywire

With repeated stress and traumas over time, the parts of our body responsible for our survival start to go haywire. The cortisol and adrenaline hormones that help us run away or fight back get out of whack, the hippocampus that helps us remember past threats gets damaged, the amygdala that activates the fear response over-reacts, and the frontal cortex that turns off the fear response doesn't work the way it used to.

This results in a chronic state of anxiety, over-activation of the fear response, a withdrawal from the world in an attempt to deal with our fears, and a general lack of adaptation to the world:

- The soldier who returns from Iraq looks for the switch to turn off his combat reaction, but he doesn't find it because it doesn't exist.

- The woman who was a victim of rape tries to "move on" with her life and start to date men again, but she is overcome with anxiety and fear, and cannot stand to have people get close to her, literally.

These are all situations where PTSD sufferers cannot just will away their responses because the responses are ingrained into their brains and bodily response systems. They can't just "get over it," because it is not in their power to do so.

So what should they do?

How to Start to Move On From Psychological Trauma

The first step on the pathway to recovery from psychological trauma is to identify the invisible barriers blocking you. We will expand upon this in the next chapter.

You then must educate yourself about what trauma is and the corrosive and subtle ways it can affect you. We will work on that more in the chapter after that. Many of these things you might read about and say, hey that describes me! The lesson is that it is not your fault for not getting over it.

But don't worry. Help is on the way.

CHAPTER 4: BARRIERS TO RECOVERY

This chapter is about the barriers you may encounter on your path toward recovery from psychological trauma. These barriers can take many forms, and aren't always easy to identify right away.

As we discussed in the last chapter, if not dealt with correctly, trauma leads to changes in the brain that make the painful memories keep coming back when they are least expected. To get rid of these painful memories and the emotions that flood the body, people initiate evasive maneuvers. They drink or take drugs to dampen down the feelings, to eliminate the stress hormone responses and to blot out the painful memories. But these behaviors can become barriers in your path toward recovery from psychological trauma.

Research has shown that alcohol and drugs, like heroin, or related pain killers, like oxycodone, sedating benzodiazepine drugs (Xanax, Valium), and marijuana, actually reduce the stress hormones and make stress systems better…in the short term. The problem is that sooner or later these effects go away, and then the trauma victim is left with the stress symptoms again… along with a hangover, and maybe a DUI, addiction, or a pink slip.

Some people may work all the time, or lose themselves in endless affairs, or find other activities to distract their minds from their traumas. These people go to extraordinary ends to avoid their memories, but they are fighting against the tide, because trauma has changed their neurological systems. In effect, they are fighting against their own mind, brain, and body.

All of these ways to try and get away from the trauma are ultimately barriers to your recovery.

You Can Run, But You Can't Hide

When my father could not address the trauma of my mother's death, he set the course for a long-term path that would affect my siblings and me for the rest of our lives. One of my sisters ran away from home at the age of sixteen and never came back. My brother dropped out of his first year of college when he was eighteen and I was twelve. He left home, and I didn't see him again for another six years. During that time, he drifted around the country, working odd jobs, often without a permanent address, and finally enlisted in the Air Force, where he later obtained a higher education and went through officers' training school.

As for me, every step of my own life has been darkened by the shadow of trauma. As I explained in Chapter One, after the death of my mother, I felt sadness, guilt, and insecurity. This insecurity has plagued me for much of my life. In a variety of ways, I was told to "get over it," and I felt if I were a stronger, better person I could do just that. Because I couldn't move beyond it, because I was haunted by the memory of the loss, I felt inadequate and thus insecure.

Later in life, I poured my energies into achieving good marks in school, got into medical school, and developed a successful career. I thought I had finally moved on, gotten over the past, but the demons from my past were always there, and sooner or later I would have to deal with them. I describe how my demons finally caught up with me forty years after my personal trauma, and what happened next, in my book *The Goose That Laid the Golden Egg*, published in 2011.

The Desperate Need to Escape from Trauma

The desire to suppress the memories of the traumatic event can result in long-term harm to the psyche and/or in self-destructive behaviors we use to distance ourselves from the initial trauma. Although this struggle to suppress the traumatic memories is ultimately futile, unfortunately too many well-intentioned people — family, friends, even some professionals — who regularly counsel trauma victims to do just that: try to forget about it, or just get over it.

FIGURE 7: THE NEED TO ESCAPE

When well-intentioned people consistently advise trauma victims to forget about their traumatic experiences, those victims can easily fall into depression, substance abuse, self-loathing, or feelings of extreme inadequacy. These responses, a natural by-product for some reason of psychological trauma, are compounded by the feeling of futility and inadequacy that comes with the realization that you "can't just snap out of it."

Feelings of inadequacy and insecurity, as well as periods of free-floating anxiety, and sometimes episodes of nausea, were my personal legacy after my mother's death, but for other trauma victims, there is a different legacy. Some victims must deal with alcoholism, drug abuse, PTSD, or depression, disorders that are very common amongst trauma survivors.

It is important to note, however, that often those suffering from alcoholism, depression, extreme insecurity, and other systems resulting from a trauma DO NOT RECOGNIZE that these feelings and behaviors are the direct result of the initial trauma. Most people blindly forge on with self-destructive behaviors, with no clue about the root cause.

Although later it becomes patently obvious that these destructive behaviors are the result of the trauma, at the time, and often for many years afterward, most people do not make the connection for the following reasons:

> 1. they were so engaged in their futile attempts to flee the memories, they did not stop long enough to ask themselves why they were so self-destructive, and

> 2. it was suggested — explicitly and implicitly — by a host of people that they were doing harmful things, not because they had experienced a bad event, but because they were bad people.

Many trauma victims fall for this line of thinking. When you are told by an authority, either directly or indirectly, whether that authority is a TV psychologist, or a teacher or a parent, that you are bad, you tend to believe the authority, especially when you get this message as a child. And once you have taken the message in, it's hard to get rid of it.

Self-Medication of Trauma

Often people go down the road of alcohol or substance abuse, not knowing that their psychological trauma was directly responsible for their problems. In the same way that people who don't know anything about trauma tell you to get over it, or snap out of it, they might tell you that your drug and drinking problems mean you're a drug addict or an alcoholic. You might enroll in drug treatment programs, or join an Alcoholics Anonymous (AA) group, but end up having a relapse.

What is the conclusion following your drug or alcohol relapse?

You're a bad person, unmotivated, or not following your program. No one will ever bring up the possibility that you have relapses when you are exposed to reminders of your trauma.

We worked with scientists at the Centers for Disease Control (CDC), our next door neighbor at Emory University in Atlanta, Georgia, and demonstrated that childhood abuse increases the risk for intravenous drug abuse in adulthood by over TEN TIMES. (It also increases the risk of cigarette smoking.) This is equivalent to the risk of getting lung cancer if you smoke cigarettes. We all know that smoking cigarettes causes lung cancer, but did we know that childhood abuse causes drug addiction?

I don't think so.

In traumatized people, PTSD and alcohol and substance abuse often occur together:

- 80% of Vietnam veterans with PTSD have a history of alcoholism or substance abuse at some time in their lives, more than double the rates seen in veterans without PTSD.

- 28% of American women with PTSD have a history of alcoholism, compared to 14% of women without PTSD (see my book *Does Stress Damage the Brain?* 2002).

Our research showed that PTSD patients abuse alcohol and substances as a form of self-medication (Bremner et al, *American Journal of Psychiatry*, 1996).

Why does trauma cause drug addiction?

You'll remember that the stress hormone adrenaline is increased in victims of psychological trauma with PTSD. Well, it turns out that some drugs, heroin being the most effective, shut off the activity of the adrenaline center in the brain located in the brain stem, called the *locus coeruleus*. Other drugs that do this include benzodiazepines, such as Valium and alcohol. Our research studies showed that PTSD patients reported that these drugs help their symptoms (cocaine makes them worse). The problem is that sooner or later the consequences of drug usage catch up with them. In any case, this clear case of heroin helping PTSD symptoms led to what we called the "self-medication hypothesis of PTSD."

So how do you recover from your addictions? Do you go to an addiction center that ignores trauma, and tries to feed you their canned program?

You can do this if you want to and you have a lot of money, but I don't think it will help you. Chances are, if you have had an addiction problem, you've already gone that route and it has failed you. You are probably reading this book because you think there might be something more, or because you have run out of options.

The truth is that until you address your trauma directly through a route such as the process in the START-NOW program, you will continue to have relapses.

Substance abuse is not the only area where trauma victims have a disconnect. Trauma victims don't make the connection between the trauma in their lives and their behavior in many ways. That is because there are so many barriers in their way.

With the tools we provide in this book, you can start to overcome those barriers, and make progress on your path toward a real recovery from psychological trauma.

The first step is to educate yourself about what effects psychological trauma has had upon you and your behavior. We will cover this in the next chapter.

CHAPTER 5: MENTAL HEALTH CONSEQUENCES OF PSYCHOLOGICAL TRAUMA: DEPRESSION AND POST-TRAUMATIC STRESS DISORDER

What happens when all your attempts at suppressing the memory of the trauma fail? What do you do then? Don't despair, because sometimes it can be the first step to recovery.

Leslie was a patient of mine who worked as a security guard in a prison. She was traumatized when one of the female inmates assaulted her. She left that job to work for an insurance company, but she continued to have problems, feeling overwhelmed and physically exhausted throughout the day. She would sleep the entire weekend to recuperate enough to go back to work, and was unable to be intimate with her husband. As well as having symptoms of PTSD, she suffered from chronic migraine headaches and gastric ulcers.

I met with her once a week in my home office in New Haven, Connecticut, when I was an Assistant Professor of Psychiatry at the Yale University School of Medicine. In addition to my research and teaching activities, I spent a few hours a week seeing patients with PTSD and depression who were struggling with recovery from psychological trauma.

Our home was in a leafy neighborhood of large, stately old homes a few blocks from the Yale campus, once the homes of the leading citizens of the city, but had since fallen on hard times. Many of them were used as dorms by a Catholic College across the street. Since then, however, due to the efforts of renovation-minded urban pioneers such as ourselves, the neighborhood was making a comeback.

Initially our psychotherapy treatment focused on the trauma of the assault. However, one night, as the daylight filtered through the window and the darkness of late autumn entered my office, she recalled a previously suppressed memory of something bad that happened in childhood. Apparently, her grandfather had sexually abused her.

She didn't have the opportunity to deal with her trauma earlier because she didn't have the right forum to discuss her feelings. She felt a conflict about revealing the abuse perpetrated by her grandfather to her parents. It is also possible that her own parents were not willing to hear terrible news about their daughter's abuse by their own parent. Since this trauma could not be expressed verbally, it came out in other ways.

The chronic stress of the trauma and keeping the secret led to long-term changes in her stress hormone systems. Repeated increases in cortisol caused by events that would remind her of the trauma led to thinning of the lining of the stomach resulting in her gastric ulcers. She also developed a number of other physical symptoms related to increased stress hormones, such as upset stomach, headache, problems with memory and concentration, and excessive fatigue.

Only when she faced another traumatic stressor (the assault) did her defenses become so weak that she could no longer suppress the memories of the sexual abuse she experienced as a child.

With time, we were able to go back and re-write her history, to incorporate what happened to her, so that she no longer needed to invest so much energy in walling off parts of her memories.

As the above story illustrates, victims are often able to contain their traumatic memories until a further stressor weakens their defense systems. Certainly, that occurred in my case.

The Stress of Duke Medical School

I was a twenty-five-year-old student at Duke University School of Medicine, in Durham, North Carolina, and I was coming unglued. Under the enormous stress and competition of med school, all my insecurities and never resolved hurt could no longer be contained. Like many trauma victims, rather than deal directly with the pain of my mother's death, I tried just not to think about it, to get over it.

For years, I pushed the bad feelings and memories away, until stress dissolved my defenses. In the same way, my Vietnam vet who was a firefighter in Vietnam did great until he had to rescue some kids from a burning house—that stressor broke down his mental defenses.

Now that I was under the maximum stress of Duke Med, I couldn't do that any longer. I was falling apart. By the third year, I was so burned out that I felt I had to go home, back to my native Washington state, to recharge my batteries.

You Can't Go Home Again

When I got home, I realized, in effect, that "home" did not exist. It was like the title of the book by the novelist, Thomas Wolfe, *You Can't Go Home Again.*

Normally, we ground ourselves in the past. Where we come from, our core moral values, our family history, give us our identity, our sense of security and peace. That is what we call home. But I didn't have that. My family history was traumatic.

As a result of my traumatic past, the core of myself, the collection of memories of my childhood, were painful and distorted. So I was stuck. I couldn't move forward because I could no longer stand the pressure, but I was afraid to go back because of the pain associated with the past. Something in me knew, however, that if I didn't go back and look at the past, there was no way I could move forward.

Facing the Past

So for the first time, instead of running away from my memories, I faced them. I faced them literally when I came upon a box in the basement of my childhood home. There I found a photograph album. I opened it and saw a picture of my parents, very young, dressed in white, together holding a knife used to cut a wedding cake. It was the first picture I had seen of my mother in years. She was stunning.

Another photo showed my parents sitting on the hood of a 56 Chevy with tall Washington State Douglas Firs behind them, drinking together out of a milk carton. I found yet another picture of my mother in a plain dress holding a baby (my sister) with the solid gold wheat fields of the Dakota prairie as a background.

The image I had of my mother was that of a difficult woman who was messy and who didn't clean up after herself or her children, but here I saw a beautiful woman in her prime who looked as if she loved her children and who took great care of herself and them.

It dawned on me then that perhaps I had the wrong image of my mother all this time, and that if the memory of my mother was distorted, perhaps other memories were equally inaccurate.

Re-Writing the Past: My Story

With that one box, I realized that I had to go back, search for the real truth and then rewrite the memories that were holding me back. I began the process by getting information from photographs, relatives, and friends. This information helped me to modify the beliefs I had wrongly held about the events and about myself. The information also helped me to come to terms, for the first time, with the painful memories and feelings I had been pushing away for years.

I later re-wrote the history of my own history (including the background story) in my book *The Goose That Laid the Golden Egg*, originally published in 2011 and released in a 2nd edition in 2014. By doing so, I followed the "R" in START; namely, Re-visit the scene of your trauma and "Re-write" your own history, but this time do it on your own terms. We cover the "R" in START in more detail later.

However, if I can do it, you can do it, too.

Betsy Re-Writes the Past

Traumatic memories are often not only distorted, but also supercharged with emotion. I had a patient named Betsy who illustrates this point well.

Betsy was raped as a teenager, and after that, every time she had physical contact with a man, she felt intense fear and anxiety. This made it very difficult for her to have close relationships with men. But since she wanted to have the intimate relationship that comes with sexual relations, she would force herself to go through with intercourse. How? She would mentally dissociate or use alcohol or drugs to decrease her anxiety.

This woman was suffering from an inability to turn off the fear response, even when there was no true threat.

Because of her rape experience, she automatically associated the sensation of being touched with a life threat for years after the original event.

As we indicated in Chapter 2, the fear memory is stored in a part of the brain called the amygdala. Another part of the brain, called the frontal cortex, is responsible for extinction of fear. In time, when it becomes clear   there is no true threat associated with the experience, the frontal cortex will inhibit the fear responses coming from the amygdala.

But in some trauma victims, the frontal cortex doesn't turn on properly, and the fear response keeps coming from the amygdala, again and again. These responses are automatic, and the trauma victim has no control over them.

For Betsy to move beyond her predicament, she had to re-write her memories related to intimacy with men. Her treatment involved a detailed exploration through psychotherapy of all of the thoughts, feelings, and ideas   in her mind at the time of the original rape. We explored her intense fear, the physical sensations that accompanied the rape, some of the thoughts that were going through her mind. It was necessary for her to learn as much as possible about what had actually happened, to re-visit issues about whether there was anything she could have done to avoid the rape. Re-writing the memory also involved re-exposing herself to being touched by a man, and in essence replacing the fear-memory associated with the rape with the positive memory associated with being with a man who was bringing pleasure instead of victimization.

Trauma Spectrum Disorders

Trauma can have a number of effects on the individual; in more extreme versions the effects can rise to the level of a mental disorder.

These disorders were described as trauma-spectrum disorders in the book *Does Stress Damage the Brain?* They include PTSD, some anxiety disorders, depression, dissociative disorders, borderline personality disorder, alcoholism, substance abuse, and somatization (conversion of anxiety into physical symptoms) disorders.

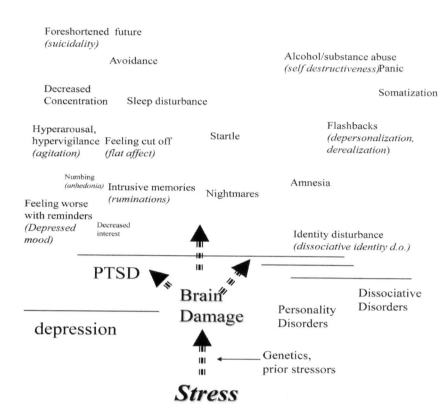

FIGURE 8: TRAUMA SPECTRUM DISORDERS

Trauma leads to a range of symptoms and the symptoms of trauma-related mental disorders often overlap with each other. For instance, in the diagram above, everything the line over "depression" are symptomsm of depression, those above the line over "PTSD" are symptoms of PTSD. As can be seen, the PTSD symptom of feeling cut off from others can be reframed as the depression symptom of flat affect, and so on. This demonstrates that trauma-related mental disorders are not discrete disorders, but rather a spectrum of symptoms with some traumatized persons exhibiting more of one core of symptoms than another. Adapted from figure in *Does Stress Damage the Brain?* (see Appendix C for permissions).

If you have one of these trauma-spectrum psychiatric disorders, you may need to augment working the START-NOW program and using tools for coping with stress that we outline later in this book, things you can do on your own by seeking out professional assessment and treatment from qualified mental health providers.

Major Depression

Psychological trauma can lead to a mental disorder called major depression. Depression is very common, affecting 15% of people at some time in their lives (Kessler, R.C., 2003, JAMA – see Bibliography in Appendix D).

The cost of lost productivity related to depression in the United States is 31 billion dollars every year (WF Stewart et al, 2003, JAMA), not only because people call in sick, but also because they show up at work and basically spend about three hours doing nothing because they are too depressed. Less than a third of these people, however, are being treated for their depression.

Symptoms of Major Depression

If you feel depressed most of the day every day or have trouble concentrating or focusing, you may suffer from depression. This may be associated with thoughts that you would be better off dead, or active plans to kill yourself, a loss of energy, appetite, and interest in things. You may have a loss of interest in sex, or in doing things that you used to like to do.

Depression is associated with problems with memory and sleeping, and feeling hopeless and worthless. You may have crying spells for no reason, or feel like life is not worth living. If depression affects someone you know, it may seem like they are focusing on something related to their family or personal life in a negative way, but it may be depression driving their behavior.

DSM CRITERIA FOR MAJOR DEPRESSION

A. At least five of the following symptoms have been present during the same two-week period, and represent a change from previous functioning (one of the symptoms is either a depressed mood or loss of interest or pleasure):

1. Depressed mood most of the day, nearly every day, as indicated either by subjective reports (e.g., feels sad or empty) or observations made by others (e.g., appears tearful)
2. Markedly diminished interest or pleasure in all, or almost all, activities most of the day, nearly every day (as indicated either by subjective account or observations made by others)
3. Significant weight loss when not dieting or weight gain (e.g., a change of more than 5% of body weight in a month), or decrease or increase in appetite nearly every day
4. Insomnia or hypersomnia nearly every day
5. Psychomotor agitation or retardation nearly every day (observable by others, not merely subjective feelings of restlessness or being slowed down)
6. Fatigue or loss of energy nearly every day
7. Feelings of worthlessness or excessive or inappropriate guilt (which may be delusional) nearly every day (not merely self-reproach or guilt about being sick)
8. Diminished ability to think or concentrate, or indecisiveness, nearly every day (either by subjective accounts or as observed by others)
9. Recurrent thoughts of death (not just fear of dying), recurrent suicidal ideation without a specific plan, or a suicide attempt or specific plan for committing suicide.

B. The symptoms do not meet the criteria for a mixed episode (i.e., with manic symptoms included).

C. The symptoms cause clinically significant distress or impairment in social, occupational, or other important areas of functioning.

D. The symptoms are not due to the direct physiological effects of a substance (e.g., a drug of abuse, a medication) or a general medical condition.

E. The symptoms are not better accounted for by bereavement, i.e., after the loss of a loved one, the symptoms persist for longer than two months or are characterized by marked functional impairment, morbid preoccupation with worthlessness, suicidal ideation, psychotic symptoms, or psychomotor retardation.

FIGURE 9: DSM CRITERIA FOR MAJOR DEPRESSION

Post-traumatic Stress Disorder

Another possible consequence of psychological trauma is post-traumatic stress disorder (PTSD).

When we first started our inpatient treatment unit for PTSD at the West Haven, CT, Veterans Administration Hospital, back in 1988, the U.S. Congress awarded us a grant to establish the National Center for PTSD. Our site was the neuroscience research division.

PTSD was first established as a psychiatric diagnosis in 1980; before that time the medical profession did not recognize that stressful or traumatic events could lead to a psychiatric disorder. We thought that if you had symptoms like PTSD, they were probably related to some other cause—like a bad personality.

This approach is obviously wrong-headed, and not helpful. We have come a long way since that time, but in 1988, most psychiatrists didn't believe in or use the diagnosis of PTSD.

We performed a review of the medical charts at the VA Hospital, and found that none of the patients in our treatment program had ever been diagnosed or treated for PTSD. Their histories were that they came to the VA maybe once in the twenty years after the war, were misdiagnosed as having schizophrenia or some other malady unrelated to the combat experiences, got frustrated, and went back to wherever they came from.

Now we literally had people coming out of the woods, people who had lived in trailers in the remote corners of rural Connecticut with no running water or electricity. When they heard about the availability of a specific treatment for their complaints, they sought it out.

We know a lot more about PTSD today than we did in 1988. That is because we have had more focused treatments, but also because of the research we've performed.

- More than half of Americans will experience a traumatic event at some time in their lives.

- For women the most common type of trauma is sexual abuse or assault, and for men it is physical assault.

- 30% of combat veterans from the Vietnam War developed PTSD within the first few months of the war, and it became chronic in 15%.

- These statistics are pretty standard for all types of trauma, and in men and women.

- 8% of all Americans have PTSD at some time in their lives, and for reasons that are unclear, it is twice as common in women as it is in men (Kessler RC, Arch Gen Psychiatry, 2005).

A history of prior trauma predisposes you to do worse in terms of PTSD. If you were abused as a child, a rape is more likely to lead to PTSD. Similarly, in a study we published in *The American Journal of Psychiatry* in 1993, we found that veterans abused as children were four times more likely to develop PTSD in Vietnam, even if they were totally normal when they went overseas.

Not all people exposed to the same level of trauma develop PTSD, although there is a clear relationship between severity and repetition of trauma and risk of developing PTSD. I usually tell people that it is like the relationship between radiation and the risk of developing cancer; the greater your radiation exposure over the course of your life, the greater your risk of developing cancer. However given any two people with the same level of radiation exposure, one person may develop cancer while the other does not. This difference may be related to genetics and other factors that we don't understand.

Post-traumatic stress disorder (PTSD) is by definition linked to a traumatic event. As well, addition you need a minimum number of symptoms from a Chinese menu.

There are three groups of symptoms of PTSD; namely, intrusions, avoidance, and hyper arousal. You need to have one from the first group, three from the second, and two from the third, as well as a significant impairment in work and/or social function to meet criteria for the diagnosis.

If you have recurrent memories of the traumatic event that you cannot control, nightmares, feeling worse with reminders, increased physiological responding to reminders (increased heart rate and blood pressure) or feeling as if the traumatic event were recurring in your physical responses, these are all intrusive symptoms of PTSD.

Many Iraq veterans have increased physiological responding and anxiety when they see something benign like a bag of garbage by the side of the road because this reminds them of Intermittent Explosive Devices (IEDs) often hidden in bags of garbage by the side of the road and detonated by insurgents in Iraq when the armored vehicles drove by on patrols. Fear related to IEDs can turn a simple trip to the grocery store into a terrifying experience.

The second group of symptoms of PTSD are avoidance. These include avoiding things that would remind you of the trauma, or attempts to avoid thinking about the trauma (whether it is childhood abuse, a car accident, or combat in Iraq or Afghanistan). Having trouble remembering an important aspect of a combat event, or having a decrease in interest in things you used to like to do (e.g., you don't like to play sports, or you don't want to go out to the movies) are aspects of avoidance. Other avoidance symptoms include feeling detached or cut off from others, feeling emotionally numb, or having a sense of foreshortened future. As part of their avoidance, PTSD patients might feel uncomfortable in crowds, and may have trouble just getting out of the house.

The third group of symptoms is hyper-arousal. Symptoms of hyper-arousal include trouble falling or staying asleep, irritability, outbursts of anger, and difficulty concentrating. An increased startle response; for example, being jumpy with loud noises, is another symptom of hyper-arousal, as are symptoms of hyper-vigilance.

In the recently released DSM-5, symptoms of PTSD have remained mostly the same, but the trauma definition no longer requires feelings of fear, helplessness, or horror in conjunction with the trauma (American Psychiatric Association, 2013). In addition, new qualifying symptoms were added. These include a new criterion of negative alterations in cognition and mood which comprises many different symptoms, including new ones such as a persistent and distorted blame of self or others, and a persistent negative emotional state. A new symptom of reckless or destructive behavior was also added as part of the hyper-arousal symptom cluster. The DSM-5 has overall loosened the criteria for PTSD, so that a much larger proportion of the population is expected to meet criteria for PTSD under the new definition.

Trauma is Trauma is Trauma

In the course of my working career, I have moved from working with veterans, to childhood abuse survivors, and eventually to patients with a wide variety of traumas. When I first started out, I didn't even make the connection between my own personal experiences and those of my patients. At that time we thought of "combat trauma" as distinct from "rape trauma" or other types of traumas.

As I started to give lectures to people in different countries, I realized that every country and every trauma group felt they were unique. I started out as an "American Vietnam Combat Trauma" expert, and went to England, where they had recently discovered "Falkland Islands War Trauma." In the Netherlands, it was "Indonesian War of Independence", Japan was "Tsunami Survivors", Italy was focused on childhood abuse, and in Armenia, the earthquake survivors.

In the US, we had experts focused on rape trauma, childhood abuse, the Holocaust, Vietnam, and hurricane, and car accident victims. There was also a focus on battered woman's syndrome. No one was able to accept that the effects of the traumas on the individual were equivalent. The effects of any type of trauma not specific to the person were thought to have nothing to do with them.

DSM CRITERIA FOR POST-TRAUMATIC STRESS DISORDER

A. The person has been exposed to a traumatic event where the person experienced, witnessed, or was confronted with an event that involved actual or threatened death or serious injury, or a threat to the physical integrity of self or others.

B. The traumatic event is persistently re-experienced in one (or more) of the following ways:

1. Recurrent and intrusive distressing recollections of the event, including images, thoughts, or perceptions.

2. Recurrent distressing dreams of the event.

3. Acting or feeling as if the traumatic event were recurring (includes a sense of reliving the experience, illusions, hallucinations, and dissociative flashback episodes, including those that occur on awakening or when intoxicated). Note: In young children, trauma-specific reenactment may occur.

4. Intense psychological distress at exposure to internal or external cues that symbolize or resemble an aspect of the traumatic event.

5. Physiological reactivity on exposure to internal or external cues that symbolize or resemble an aspect of the traumatic event.

C. Persistent avoidance of stimuli associated with the trauma and numbing of general responsiveness (not present before the trauma), as indicated by three (or more) of the following:

1. Efforts to avoid thoughts, feelings, or conversations associated with the trauma

2. Efforts to avoid activities, places, or people that arouse recollections of the trauma

3. Inability to recall an important aspect of the trauma

4. Markedly diminished interest or participation in significant activities

5. Feeling of detachment or estrangement from others

6. Restricted range of affect (e.g., unable to have loving feelings)

7. Sense of a foreshortened future (e.g., does not expect to have a career, marriage, children, or a normal life span)

D. Persistent symptoms of increased arousal (not present before the trauma), as indicated by two (or more) of the following:

1. Difficulty falling or staying asleep

2. Irritability or outbursts of anger

3. Difficulty concentrating

4. Hypervigilance

5. Exaggerated startle response

E. Duration of the disturbance is more than 1 month.

F. The disturbance causes clinically significant distress or impairment in social, occupational, or other important areas of functioning.

Specify if: Acute: if duration of symptoms is less than 3 months, or Chronic: if duration of symptoms is 3 months or more, or With delayed onset: if onset of symptoms is at least six months after the stressor.

Other Anxiety Disorders Related to Psychological Trauma

Another potential consequence of exposure to traumatic stress is anxiety and panic disorder.Panic disorder is characterized by episodes of extreme anxiety or panic that come out of the blue and make people feel as though they're going to die or go crazy. Associated symptoms include rapid heart rate, feeling as though you can't breathe, muscle tension, nausea, constricted feeling in the chest or throat, sweating, dizziness, and feeling as if you're out of your body or unreal.

Sometimes people with panic disorder have a fear of having an anxiety reaction in public places, in crowds, or while going over a bridge. This can lead to a fear of leaving the house, called agoraphobia, which literally means fear of the marketplace in Greek. Agoraphobia can be very disabling.

Anxiety Disorder Not Otherwise Specified (NOS) means symptoms of anxiety that are disabling but don't fit into one of the other anxiety disorders. These symptoms can include free-floating anxiety associated with trouble breathing, chest pain, nausea, and stomach discomfort. This is another possible outcome of exposure to psychological trauma.

The Effects of Psychological Trauma That Cannot Be Measured

Psychological trauma has lasting effects on the individual not easily captured in our psychiatric diagnostic categories. These include the effects of trauma on the individual's perception of society, the world, and the meaning of their relationship with the world and with others.

The psychiatric disorder, PTSD, is perhaps unique in representing interplay between psychiatric and neurological disease, and a profound alteration in the individual's existential view of the world and his or her place in it. Trauma victims frequently suffer from "survivor's guilt," the feeling that the individual should not have survived when so many others died.

The bare fact that the person survived when so many others perished adds to the feeling that the world is meaningless and nothing makes sense. Victims believe they do not deserve to "leave all of this behind them" and "get on with their life" when only chance led to their survival while others did not survive. They may feel they have more in common with the dead than the living, and that the living do not understand how they feel. This line of thinking can lead to depression and despair, alienation and ultimately suicide and death.

In the next few chapters, we review other consequences of psychological trauma, including borderline personality disorder (BPD), the dissociative disorders, the functional pain disorders, and somatization disorders. We also review how psychological trauma impacts on physical health.

CHAPTER 6: BORDERLINE PERSONALITY DISORDER AND THE DISSOCIATIVE DISORDERS

Borderline personality disorder (BPD) and the Dissociative Disorders are both mental disorders that are frequently associated with a history of childhood stress. Although BPD is currently grouped with other personality disorders in the DSM, like narcissistic personality disorder and avoidant personality disorder, it is one of the psychiatric disorders that were grouped in the trauma spectrum disorders in the book *Does Stress Damage the Brain?* because of its connection with childhood trauma. Even in people without a clear history of trauma, a careful interview often shows that there is a history of emotional abuse, or something about the parent-child interaction in childhood that likely contributes to the disorder. Dissociative disorders are often linked to a history of severe early childhood physical and/or sexual abuse, and were also grouped in the trauma spectrum disorders.

Borderline Personality Disorder (BPD) Defined

BPD is characterized by an intense fear of abandonment by other persons. This results in an instability of interpersonal relationships because the person with BPD desperately tries to pull other people in their lives closer to them, even if it requires a negative strategy to do so. People with BPD also have problems with self-image, mood swings, and impulsive and self-destructive behavior. BPD starts in early adulthood, and can last for months or years. People often get better with time. No two cases are the same.

BPD patients sometimes cut themselves, often repeatedly, for reasons that are not entirely understood. However, a lot of BPD patients will say things like they wanted to replace their inner psychic pain with a physical pain, or that they have an intense feeling of inner emptiness or an uncomfortable feeling that is so unbearable that the only thing that will break it is to cut themselves. Many BPD patients end up with scars on their arms and legs.

These people can damage themselves in other ways, like reckless driving, reckless spending, wild and uncontrolled sex, drugs or drinking, or binge eating. Life with someone with BPD can be a roller coaster ride; you never know what's going to happen next. That's because people with BPD create dramas as a way to prevent people from abandoning them (even if that's totally unrealistic) or to distract themselves from their intense feelings of inner emptiness:

- They do things like make repeated suicide threats or attempts.

- Their mood can swing all over the place.

- They have outbursts of intense anger and irritability.

- Sometimes they have dissociative symptoms, which we describe later in this chapter.

Although people like BPD might seem like they are actors in a Tennessee Williams play, and that that they should just pull themselves together, the fact is they have little control over themselves. They can't just "snap out of it". Believe us, we have a lot of experience with this disorder. Coming back to Planet Earth for BPD patients is a long process that requires them to follow the steps of the recovery process outlined in this book. But don't give up, there is hope.

Relationship Between BPD and Psychological Trauma

The link between Borderline Personality Disorder (BPD) and some form of trauma in childhood is clear. Over half of people with BPD were sexually abused in childhood. The risk of developing BPD is increased five-fold after exposure to childhood trauma. About half of BPD patients also have PTSD, while half of PTSD patients have BPD. When BPD patients also have PTSD, they tend to do worse.

Like PTSD patients, BPD patients with a history of childhood trauma have smaller hippocampal volumes and dysfunction in the frontal cortex. We found that BPD patients with early trauma did not react physiologically to reminders of their childhood trauma, but they had huge reactions when read a hypothetical story about a child being abandoned in a shopping mall. This is amazing biological evidence that their fear of abandonment is real, and is wired in the brain (although not necessarily permanently, as we will discuss in later chapters on the recovery process from psychological trauma). We think that this comes from something that went wrong in early childhood related to how they form attachments to other people, most importantly the people who took care of them (i.e., Moms and Dads). This could be due to physical or sexual abuse, or more likely emotional abuse, or even just a bad fit between parent and child for whatever reason. That means that BPD is probably not your fault, although that doesn't mean you can just sit back and wait for someone else to fix it. The key to your recovery lies within yourself, and we give you the tools in this book to find that key and open the door to your recovery.

Dissociative Disorders as a Consequence of Psychological Trauma

Another group of psychiatric disorders that are often linked to psychological trauma, usually in early childhood, are the dissociative disorders. Dissociation is defined as a breakdown in memory, identity, and consciousness.

In common speech, the terms "dissociation" and "disassociation" are often used interchangeably. However, when we talk about psychological trauma, dissociation has a specific meaning for us. It does not mean to disassociate, which is to say you don't want to have anything to do with someone, because, for example, they are a Republican. Our meaning of dissociation is a particular set of experiences that are often seen following exposure to psychological trauma.

Dissociative symptoms include:

- amnesia — gaps in memory not due to ordinary forgetting;

- depersonalization — out-of-body experiences and other distortions of the sense of one's own body, such as feelings that your arms are like toothpicks or your body is very large;

- derealization — distortions in visual perception, such as seeing things as if they are in a tunnel, things are in black and white or colors are very bright, distortions in time, like the feeling that time stands still or is moving very fast, and

- identity disturbance — fragmentation of the sense of the self.

Current DSM-IV dissociative disorders include Dissociative Identity Disorder (DID), Depersonalization Disorder, Dissociative

Amnesia, and Dissociative Disorder not Otherwise Specified (DDNOS) (which includes fugue states and derealization disorders, and is sort of a grab bag term for people with disabling dissociative symptoms that don't really fit into any other group).

The Fragmentation of Personality in Dissociative Identity Disorder

Dissociative Identity Disorder (DID) (originally called multiple personality disorder) is characterized by a number of dissociative symptoms as well as disturbances in normal identity. The identity disturbance of DID is really related to a series of amnestic episodes, which when extreme can lead the patient to feel as though there are multiple facets of themselves that are imperfectly connected with one another. The different personality states are often experienced in a dreamy, dissociative state.

DID was previously termed "multiple personality disorder," remember from popular movies like *The Three Faces of Eve*, but the name was changed by the American Psychiatric Association to emphasize the identity fragmentation that occurs in these people. The name change is also in response to extensive media attention, which has focused on the "either/or" aspect of whether an individual has one personality or more than one.

In my clinical work, we have not found this type of dichotomous thinking to be helpful in treating traumatized patients with identity disturbances. Typically, patients describe identity fragments to which they may have attached a name label, and which may have different levels of development but are not completely formed into distinct personalities in the same way that we would think of normal personality. Some of the identity fragments may be associated with painful memories (e.g., a six-year-old fragment who was sexually abused, is very angry, and carries the feelings of fear and shame), whereas others are protected from these painful memories (a ten-year-old "good girl" who is happy and polite).

The identity fragments in DID patients, however, are all part of the same person. As the psychiatrist Colin Ross MD wrote in his book, *Dissociative Identity Disorder*, ultimately it is not possible to have "multiple personalities." Rather, it is the perception of traumatized patients that they have distinct identity fragments within themselves. These identity fragments may play a role in avoiding painful memories of trauma that can incapacitate the individual in his or her daily life. However, ultimately patients need to come to terms with their painful memories and realize that all of the identity fragments are part of just one person.

People often experience traumatic events in a dissociated state. Later, even minor stressors can make them dissociate, or they may dissociate when something reminds them of the original trauma.

Acute Stress Disorder

Acute Stress Disorder (ASD) replaced acute PTSD, which was part of the DSMIIIR and which described episodes of PTSD that occurred during the first month after trauma (since PTSD required a minimum duration of one month of symptoms).

In addition to requiring the presence of a traumatic event, ASD required three of five dissociative symptoms (numbing, derealization, depersonalization, amnesia, or being "in a daze"); one or more of each of the PTSD re-experiencing, avoidance, and hyper arousal symptoms; and functional disturbance (as in DSM-IV PTSD). Most people with ASD go on to develop PTSD.

Dissociation in Response to Trauma

When people dissociate after trauma it can be a sign that things are not going so well. Our studies showed that Vietnam veterans who dissociated at the time of combat trauma were more likely to develop PTSD later, and continued to have dissociative responses to subsequent stressors (Bremner, J. Douglas et al., American Journal of Psychiatry, 1992).

We found that Vietnam combat veterans with PTSD had increased dissociative symptom levels compared to combat veterans without PTSD:

- 86% of patients in a group of Vietnam veterans with PTSD in an inpatient treatment program had the diagnosis of a dissociative disorder, whereas

- Essentially 100% of patients with dissociative identity disorder (DID) in a different inpatient program had a history of severe childhood abuse and the diagnosis of PTSD.

To conduct studies of treatment and neurobiology of dissociation, we developed a scale for use as a repeated measure of dissociative states (mentioned above): the Clinician Administered Dissociative States Scale (CADSS).

The CADSS is a nineteen-item scale administered by a clinician who begins each question with the phrase "at this time" and then reads the item to the subject. The subject then endorses one of a range of possible responses: 0 not at all, 1 slightly, 2 moderately, 3 considerably, 4 extremely.

Some of the dissociative symptoms measured with the CADSS that were most commonly endorsed in traumatized patients included

- "Did things seem to be moving in slow motion?"

- "Did sounds change, so that that they became very soft or very loud?" and

- "Did it seem as if you were looking at things as an observer or a spectator?"

We found that these symptoms increased when PTSD patients were re-exposed to reminders of their original trauma during a traumatic memories group I conducted at the inpatient PTSD program at the VA hospital.

Dissociation and Psychosis

Sometimes dissociative symptoms can resemble symptoms of psychosis, like seeing things that are not there or hearing voices, even the perception of the voice of a dead person whom the victim of psychological trauma once knew.

Dissociation, however, is usually related to a traumatic event, whereas psychotic symptomatology does not show such a specific connection with trauma.

Psychotic auditory hallucinations, on the other hand, commonly consist of an unrecognized foreign voice with specific types of content, such as making disparaging comments about the individual. Finally, visual hallucinations in dissociative disorders are related to the traumatic memory and involve the perception of normal "intact" scenes, whereas psychotic visual hallucinations have bizarre content and often involve a breakdown of the scenario of the scene.

Dissociation and Trauma: A Case Study

One of the best ways to understand the symptoms of dissociation is to look at the story of someone who is affected by them.

I once had a patient named Chuck who was a combat veteran in the Vietnam War. He said that after a fire fight, they moved in to kill off the enemy with bayonets. They stabbed the enemy rather than shooting them so that they would not alert the Viet Cong that they were in the area.

He said, "While we were stabbing the enemy, I felt myself drifting above the scene. I was looking at myself from a distance. That person down there was 'a Killer,' but it really wasn't me. I felt sorry for him."

This is an example of depersonalization, i.e., when you see things from outside of yourself. Other people feel distortions in their body—their arms are like toothpicks, or their body becomes very large.

I had another patient named Frank who had PTSD from Vietnam. He would be sitting on the couch next to his wife having an argument, and another person would pop up next to him, an alternative version of himself. It would be the "fighter" version of himself, ready to knife someone in the gut, or throw machine gun fire into a village without knowing who was in there—things he would not attribute to himself as things that he could easily do. He saw this person as someone different from himself.

One time he was arguing with his wife and this alternative version of himself popped up next to himself and said, "She's a bitch, hit her, she won't know the difference."

Another vet with PTSD, named Harry, used to see his buddies who died in Vietnam sitting in his car while he drove around. One day he was drinking on his back porch and he saw a helicopter landing in his back yard with his dead buddies. He saw them in a dissociated state, as though in a dream, colors were very bright, and time seemed to stand still.

His young daughter said, "Daddy, just let them go."

Later when he was drinking in his basement, they came to him. They told him to kill himself so that he could join them.

Years later, after he had completed our program, I heard that someone had pushed him in front of a subway train in New York. I never learned the details of that event.

Trauma and Development

To understand dissociative identity disorder, it is important to have an understanding of normal personality development. Almost all cases of dissociative identity disorder are related to early childhood abuse.

Childhood abuse can have lasting effects on the sense of self. Our sense of self does not exist from the time of birth; rather, it is the result of an accumulation of a lifetime's experiences and positive relationships with others. For example, a particularly positive experience with a math teacher will allow the individual to "take away" an aspect of that role model's personality, incorporate it into the sense of self, and lead to a strengthening of the personality.

A more fundamental example of this phenomenon is the interaction between infant and mother. This is what Winnicott (1965) and others who wrote about object relations theory called the phenomenon of the "good enough mother."

In abusive families, the mother may not only be not "good enough," but may actually be a source of threat. This has an important impact on the child's development of the sense of self, leading to a fragmentation of identity and a walling-off of aspects of memory and the self.

Childhood abuse can also be associated with lasting feelings of shame (related to a common process of self-blame) and rage against the perpetrator and others in the family who did not protect them. A sense of powerlessness in the face of the abuser can put the abuse victims at risk for becoming perpetrators themselves when they become adults, in an attempt to have the feeling of power over another that they could not have as children.

Based on the close relationship among dissociation, PTSD and trauma, in the book *Does Stress Damage the Brain?* I argued for a reorganization of the current diagnostic criteria for the anxiety disorders (which currently includes PTSD) and dissociative disorders. PTSD doesn't really show much in common in terms of biological changes in the brain with the other anxiety disorders, like obsessive-compulsive disorder (OCD), social phobia, generalized anxiety disorder (GAD) and panic disorder.

Research indicates that ASD and PTSD are closely related disorders. Their criteria should therefore be made consistent with one another. They should also be combined in one grouping of trauma spectrum disorders with BPD, dissociative disorders, and abuse-related depression. Like PTSD and BPD, patients with DID, or depression and a history of early abuse, also have smaller hippocampal volume on MRI scans, based on our research. This is because psychological trauma has similar effects on the brain, regardless of you psychiatric diagnosis.

We talk more about the effects of trauma on the brain and how this interacts with physical health in the next chapter.

CHAPTER 7: EFFECTS OF PSYCHOLOGICAL TRAUMA ON PHYSICAL HEALTH

Psychological trauma takes a toll on not only the mind and brain, but also the body. This can lead to a number of potentially disabling physical symptoms, like headaches, nausea, indigestion, and feelings of breathlessness, that don't always have a clear cause.

Psychological trauma can also be associated with potentially life-threatening disorders with clearly identifiable physical abnormalities, including cancer, heart disease, gastric ulcers and diabetes.

Finally, the functional pain disorders are defined as disorders with specific symptoms where an underlying medical cause is not easy to find. These disorders, which are very common, are often seen in people with a history of psychological trauma, although a trauma history is not necessary for their development. Functional pain disorders include irritable bowel syndrome (IBS), fibromyalgia, non-specific low back pain, chronic pelvic pain, and temporomandibular pain around the face and jaw, and are discussed in more detail later.

Psychological trauma can also be associated with somatization disorders, described in more detail below.

Stress and Heart Disease

Heart disease is the most common cause of death in the United States, and psychological trauma contributes to the development of heart disease in many people. The ancient Greeks, as well as many other cultures throughout history, believed the heart was the source of emotion. This idea has carried over into statements about someone dying of a broken heart, and similar expressions. The fact is this popular wisdom may not be so far from the truth.

Research done by us and others showed that emotional factors, including exposure to psychological trauma, play a role in heart disease. Repeated or chronic stress can have a wearing response on the heart, immune function, and metabolism of glucose, leading to chronic elevations in blood pressure and heart rate, problems with immune responses to infections, and elevations in blood sugar that may lead to diabetes. This is in part related to chronic elevations of the stress hormones, cortisol and adrenaline.

Psychological trauma makes you more reactive to minor stressors in life or reminders of your trauma, especially if you have PTSD or depression. These mental processes can trigger a rapid and reversible narrowing of the blood vessels of the heart, leading to what we call ischemia, which can cause chest pain or damage to the tissues of the heart.

Stress can also cause atherosclerosis, which is a build up in the walls of the blood vessels in the heart of fats (lipids), cholesterol, and white blood cells (the cells in the body that fight infections). With time, these atherosclerotic collections can harden, which is why they are called athero (which means pudding in Greek) sclerosis (which means hardened). These atherosclerotic plaques can become brittle and break, sometimes sending a piece of plaque downstream to lodge in the narrow part of the blood vessel, blocking blood flow to a part of the heart. When that happens, it causes the heart's muscle tissue to die, leading to a heart attack, which could be fatal.

How Does Psychological Trauma Cause Heart Disease?

How is it that psychological trauma can cause a physical disorder like heart disease?

There are a number of possible ways, including the chronic elevations in cortisol and adrenaline that can lead to chronically high blood pressure and heart rate, changes in blood sugar, or changes in the peripheral nervous system that controls the heart and blood vessels. Animal studies show that chronic stress actually damages the inside of the blood vessels of the heart, probably due to excessively high levels of adrenaline. Psychological trauma also affects immune function, which can affect the heart, leading to an increase in heart disease in people with PTSD and depression related to psychological trauma.

Based on our research, we think that psychological trauma leads to an over-reaction of the blood vessels, so that the muscles in the wall of the blood vessels become over-reactive. This can cause a stress-induced narrowing that decreases blood flow to certain parts of the heart, resulting in ischemia (which is a lessening of blood flow to a particular part of the body), and possibly heart attacks.

Increase in Heart Disease with Natural Disasters

When there is an emotionally stressful event, like natural or industrial disasters, or terrorist attacks, there is an increase in heart disease. This can be seen in an increase in admissions to the hospital for chest pain and heart attacks (see the chapter "Heart Disease and Depression" by Vaccarino and Bremner in Appendix D). Even things like major sporting events have been associated with an increase in admissions to the hospital for heart disease. For instance,

- In the week after the Northridge earthquake in the Los Angeles area in 1994, there was a 35% increase in people admitted to the hospital for heart attacks, and a five-fold increase in sudden cardiac deaths.

- After the World Trade Center terrorist attack in New York City on September 11, 2001, there was a 50% increase in heart disease in New York over the next three years.

Other studies show that people who've had a short-term increase in work load, such as a high pressure deadline, have a six-fold increase in the risk of having a heart attack during the next day.

Sudden stressors, even something like a surprise birthday party, can "stun" the heart, causing it to pump blood abnormally for a short period of time.

Studying the Effects of Stress on the Heart in the Laboratory

One thing we do in our research program at Emory University in Atlanta, GA, is see how people with heart disease react to stress. To do this, we bring them into the laboratory to do what we call a "mental stress test," using complicated and difficult things like having them do hard math problems, make speeches, or solve puzzles under time pressure. We then measure blood flow in the heart with a scanner.

Mental stress can cause a reduction in blood flow in the heart, or ischemia, in some people, in the same way that physical exercise can. At least one third of heart disease patients get ischemia during mental stress, usually without feeling any pain.

Even simple stresses of daily life can make the heart ischemic. In other words, a lot of people are walking around with potentially dangerous drops in blood flow to the heart when they get stressed out. This can happen multiple times per day, without their ever knowing about it. Our research studies showed that this is more common in people with psychological trauma in childhood and the diagnosis of PTSD or depression.

As well as ischemia, mental stress seems to affect the electrical properties of the heart. People with mental-stress-induced ischemia have an increase in heart attacks and risk of death related to a sudden stoppage of the heart due to problems with the electrical functioning of the heart. All kinds of stressors have been shown to affect heart function, including psychological trauma like childhood abuse, as well as stress at work and in the marriage, or the stress of having to care for a sick family member. These can all increase the risks of heart attacks and death from heart disease.

Functional Pain Disorders and Psychological Trauma

Psychological trauma is also associated with an increased risk for the development of functional pain disorders. These disorders are defined as ones that, after appropriate medical assessment, cannot be explained in terms of a conventionally defined medical disease based on specific biochemical or structural abnormalities.

Many times the functional pain disorders do not respond to conventional medical therapy. If you do suffer from one, though, it is important to understand the symptoms so that you can get a handle on coping with them.

Although they are usually more common in people with psychological trauma, that doesn't necessarily mean they are always caused by psychological trauma, or that there aren't other contributing factors, like things in the environment, a history of physical injury, or genetic factors. Trauma may be one of many factors that contribute to the disorders, although not likely the only one (see "Combat-related Psychiatric Syndromes" in *Functional Pain Disorders* listed in Appendix D).

Irritable Bowel Syndrome

Irritable bowel syndrome (IBS) accounts for almost half of all visits to gastroenterologists, and is one of the most common gastrointestinal diseases.

IBS is characterized by abdominal pain and discomfort and associated alterations in bowel habits with no identifiable change in the function or structure of the bowels. Similar to other functional syndromes, IBS has been defined as "symptoms not explained by structural or biochemical abnormalities" and the diagnosis has been determined by symptom criteria (e.g., pain with bowel movements).

Patients with IBS more commonly report problems with sleep, sex drive, and a loss of energy, as well as headaches, back pain, muscle pain, pain while urinating, and a feeling of urinary urgency. IBS is felt to be related to a change in how the brain communicates with the bowels, which involves both processing of emotion and how the brain regulates the bowel through the peripheral nervous system.

One theory holds that IBS is related to stress, at least in some patients. Exposure to a threat is associated with changes in bowel function in animals, including

- an increase in defecation,

- changes in colonic motility,

- changes felt to be modulated by corticotropin releasing factor (CRF), and;

- autonomic nervous system influences on the gut.

Studies have shown an increase in childhood sexual abuse trauma and exposure to general traumatic events in IBS patients. Combat veterans, especially those with PTSD, have an increase in gastrointestinal symptoms and self-reported digestive diseases. Other studies have shown that parental style, specifically hostility and rejection from paternal figures, plays a greater role in the development of IBS than childhood sexual abuse. Rates of PTSD in

IBS patients are typically higher than in the general population. An increase in symptoms of anxiety and depression, but not dissociation, has also been reported in IBS patients.

Fibromyalgia

Fibromyalgia, which affects about 5% of women and 2% percent of men, is associated with chronic widespread pain, diffuse tenderness, fatigue and sleep disturbance; diagnostic criteria require at least three months of widespread pain and pain upon digital palpation at no fewer than eleven of eighteen characteristic tender points.

Some studies have associated childhood physical abuse (but not childhood sexual abuse), or sexual assault in adulthood, with fibromyalgia. About half of fibromyalgia patients have PTSD. Fibromyalgia symptoms are also seen in at least a fifth of PTSD patients. Veterans deployed to the Gulf War had an increase in self-reported fibromyalgia (19% deployed versus 10% non-deployed).

PTSD patients with fibromyalgia symptoms have worse quality of life and more psychological distress than PTSD patients without fibromyalgia. Fibromyalgia patients also have increased rates of anxiety, depression and somatization.

Fibromyalgia is thought to be related at least in part to alterations in brain regions involved in pain and how they communicate with other parts of the body.

Low Back Pain

In the United States, back pain is the second most common symptom that drives people to go to the doctor. As with fibromyalgia and IBS, there is a lack of observable pathology to account for non-specific low back pain, treatment is difficult, and the relationship with emotional factors is not well defined.

Less than 15% of people with low back pain have an identifiable cause and treatment. This leaves a substantial proportion of people suffering back pain without any identifiable abnormality in their backs.

Prisoners of War (POWs) from Vietnam reported an increase in back problems compared to non-POW servicemen. Many returning Iraq veterans have both back pain and PTSD. They have high rates of pain related to mechanical wear and tear injuries from carrying more equipment than in prior wars (e.g., bullet proof vests) and jumping out of helicopters and armed vehicles. Low back pain and PTSD can maintain each other, with lack of mobility leading to increased avoidance, one of the symptoms of PTSD.

Chronic Pelvic Pain

Chronic pelvic pain is intermittent or continuous pain in the pelvic area that lasts at least three months.

Some people have thought of chronic pelvic pain as being a result of childhood sexual abuse. Although rates of childhood sexual trauma are higher in pelvic pain patients, exposure to childhood sexual trauma is not necessary for the development of the disorder. About half of patients with chronic pelvic pain also have PTSD. These patients also have an increase in other kinds of somatic problems.

Temporomandibular Joint Disorder (TMJD)

Temporomandibular joint disorder (TMJD) refers to pain in the jaw that can be caused by a number of factors, one of which is gnashing of teeth associated with stress. About 25% of patients with TMJD suffer from PTSD.

Somatoform Disorders

Somatoform disorders are described in the Diagnostic and Statistical Manual (DSM) of psychiatry as disorders where physical symptoms are not attributable to a known organic cause, and are not secondary to anxiety or depression. Somatization disorder involves at least eight physical symptoms in four bodily systems.

Somatization disorder patients have increased symptoms of dissociative amnesia, but not depersonalization, derealization or identify confusion or alteration. Somatization patients were found to have more history of emotional and physical abuse (but not sexual abuse) in childhood, plus more family conflict and less family cohesion.

Psychosomatic Disorders

Another term we use for all of these disorders (including the somatoform disorders and the functional pain disorders) is "psychosomatic disorders." The medical field, however, has evolved from the "it's all in your head" way of thinking to realizing that these disorders often involve a complex interchange between emotion, brain function, and function of peripheral organs, like the heart and the stomach. Multiple factors, including childhood environment, psychological trauma, physical injuries, and genetics likely play a role in these disorders.

The Complex Interplay of Stress, Mind, Brain and Body

The functional pain disorders often occur with each other and with stress-related psychiatric disorders like PTSD and depression, as well as chronic fatigue syndrome and headache. This may represent a common etiology (e.g., stress, common genetic factors, common changes in the brain), or the fact that they are involved in each other's etiology (e.g., pain leads to depression, or depression is involved in maintenance of pain after minor injury).

Sometimes symptoms of dissociation, which we reviewed in the previous chapter, are associated with functional pain syndromes. Symptoms of dissociation can resemble symptoms of a disorder called conversion disorder, which, like depersonalization, can involve distortions of how people perceive their own bodies. In conversion disorder, people may develop symptoms of losing sensation or function of an arm or leg, even though there is no identifiable medical cause. This is called "glove and stocking anesthesia," because there may be a pattern of loss of sensation that is like a glove, while the nerves are not distributed that way in the body.

Since PTSD and depression often occur with the functional pain disorders, it is likely there is some link with psychological trauma, at least in some people. However, the fact that not all patients with functional pain disorders have a history of psychological trauma, nor for that matter the diagnosis of PTSD or depression, suggests that psychological trauma is not essential for the development of chronic pain disorders.

You may or may not have a functional pain disorder. Or something like heart disease or diabetes. But the fact is that if you are reading this book, there is a good chance that psychological trauma has affected you in some way. We will continue to explore some of the ways that psychological trauma may have affected you in the next chapter.

CHAPTER 8: HOW DOES PSYCHOLOGICAL TRAUMA AFFECT *YOU* AND WHAT CAN YOU DO ABOUT IT?

If you have been traumatized and it is influencing your life (or you wonder if it has influenced your life), is there anything that can be done about it?

Yes, there is, but you shouldn't sit back and wait for someone else to do it for you.

The U.S. spends $2,100 a year on research on HIV/AIDS for every person suffering from these disorders in this country, and only $18 per person with depression. This is in spite of the fact that depression is much more common than HIV/AIDS. That means that if you are suffering from depression or PTSD related to psychological trauma, you are going to have to take charge of your recovery. As you will see in this chapter, it's better that way, anyway.

How Do You Recover from Psychological Trauma?

Trauma experts will have lots of advice to give, and it usually involves a quick fix. In my experience, however, most of these tricks will not lead to long-term results.

If you or someone close to you are trying to recover from a psychological trauma, there is hope for you. And the best person to help you recover from a traumatic stressor? YOU.

How will you go about this recovery process?

There is no single magic pill or cure, and the memories of the traumatic event will stay with you and affect you on some level for the rest of your life. Your recovery is going to take time and patience. You will experience setbacks.

But if you use the tools in this book, including the START-NOW program and the tools for coping with stress, you will get a good launch onto the path toward recovery from psychological trauma.

Educate Yourself About Psychological Trauma

To get started on that path, you need to take the first step, which is to educate yourself. Educate, educate, educate.

Knowledge is power, and the most important thing you need to do to educate yourself is learn to know yourself. That was the motto of the great Greek philosopher Socrates, who lived over 2,000 years ago, but whose words are as relevant now as they were back then.

The more we know about the potential effects psychological trauma can have on us, the better off we will be.

The starting point is this book. Learn about the symptoms of PTSD, depression, and dissociation. Educate yourself about the tools for coping with stress and the points of the START-NOW program we outline in later chapters. If you have encounters with counselors, therapists, doctors, or others, ask a lot of questions. Take notes.

Why do we think that education is so important?

Because by learning about the symptoms that can be caused by psychological trauma, including both the mental and the physical consequences, you can recognize the source. You can stop attributing things to the fact that you are evil, have a bad character, or have done something wrong, and you can recognize that your behavior is related to your life experiences.

Stop Listening to Unhelpful Advice and Negative Soundtracks

You can stop listening to unhelpful advice, like "just snap out of it" or "just get over it." It is helpful to realize the biological basis of trauma-related symptoms and difficulties in coping. You can also recognize that your feelings of being bad or evil are not based in reality, even though these types of thoughts are almost universal in trauma patients.

Childhood sexual abuse survivors may think there was something wrong with them that led to their being singled out for abuse, and their abusers may have reinforced these ideas by calling them stupid, or a slut, or a mistake, or some other negative thing. If that were the case, then why is it that car wreck survivors similarly have feelings of shame, guilt, self-doubt? It is because these are all symptoms of a disorder.

Similarly, rape survivors may feel it was their fault for having crossed that parking lot alone, or having too many beers, or going out with that guy when you should have known better, or wearing that suggestive dress. Society and the legal system reinforce these attitudes by immediately asking questions about the sexual practices of the victimized woman. Muslim countries ostracize rape victims, which causes them to deny that rape ever happened.

Overcome Your Negative Cognitions

To fight back, you need to overcome these negative thoughts.

These negative attitudes and ideas are what we call negative cognitions. The fact is that they aren't true. If the person who tormented or abused you has so much knowledge and expertise, why is it that they are going around breaking the law by committing acts of sexual abuse or physical cruelty against minors?

Many perpetrators justify their actions — they say they're teaching their children about sex — or they deny that anything ever happened. Many become very angry, vindictive and self-justified when they are accused of their crimes. Some have brought legal action, and have even won their day in court. These people can continue to do damage for years after the initial abuse or trauma. You have to learn to protect yourself from them. The first step is to get them out of your head. Those negative comments are them talking in your head, or what we call negative cognitions. It's time to get them out of there!

If you were raped in a parking lot, why is it your fault for walking alone at night? Rape is illegal, so the only person who was at fault was the rapist.

Other types of negative cognitions have to do with cause and effect. If you were in a car accident and were severely injured, that doesn't mean that every time you drive a car you will get into another accident. If you were attacked in a dark alley, that doesn't mean that every time you go into a dark place you will be attacked. You have to learn that your anxiety and fears are not reality based, and train yourself to overcome those fears.

What else can be done for trauma-related symptoms? Understanding your own symptoms and patterns of response is critical.

Protect Yourself From the Negative Consequences

If you need to take care of yourself by decreasing the stress in your life, then by all means do so. Try to recognize when your relationships are recreating the abusive pattern of the past. People tend to gravitate toward abusive relationships because they have a low sense of self-worth and think that someone who had their act together would not be interested in them if they knew what they were really like. Or maybe they recognize the defects of the other person, but fantasize about changing them.

Avoid these traps at all costs, and if you make a mistake, get out. As we discuss in a later chapter on relationships, some fundamental aspects of peoples' characters you just can't change.

Anniversary Reactions

Traumatized people often have what we call anniversary reactions linked to the time when a traumatic event happened to them; the date when their trauma occurred comes around, and they may start to feel worse.

The most famous anniversary in the United States is September 11, 2001, when terrorists flew airplanes into the World Trade Center in New York City, killing several thousand people. Thousands of people in America feel much worse around this time of year. This is one type of anniversary reaction, but anniversary reactions can come in many forms.

Many Vietnam combat veterans have an anniversary reaction around the time of year of the Tet offensive, which occurred on January 30, 1968. This was the date on which the North Vietnamese launched a massive offensive against the South Vietnamese and American forces, and has become a negative anniversary for many veterans of the Vietnam War.

Parents who lose their children have anniversary reactions for the time of their death, or maybe even their birthdays. People tend to become more symptomatic in the weeks leading up to the anniversary, and peak at the time of the anniversary. Many people don't even recognize what's happening.

So what can you do about anniversary reactions?

- First of all, recognize that they exist.

- Then prepare yourself in advance to deal with them effectively.

- Don't try and ignore it and then have them come up and smack you in the face.

- If you need to tell people in your life that this time of year is difficult, and you need to be alone more, or that you may be more difficult to live with, or you need more attention and support than usual, do it, whatever it takes.

Learn About the Relationship Between Psychological Trauma and Alcohol and Substance Abuse

Learn about the relationship between your alcohol and substance abuse and your life experiences. You may be using drugs and alcohol to numb out feelings or to help and regulate your own feelings of fear, anxiety, and depression. There may be triggers in your life that cause you to use alcohol and other substances to get things under control. You may use drugs to make it possible for yourself to have sex. These behaviors are short-term gambits that have overall negative long term consequences.

Drugs and alcohol impair your judgment and increase the chances that you will put yourself in harm's way, making it more likely that you will be re-traumatized. Although it may make you feel better in the short term, when you go through withdrawal, which is inevitable, your symptoms will be even worse. If you are under the influence of drugs or alcohol, you will not be able to follow the points of the START-NOW program.

Being impaired also makes it more likely that you cause damage to others, e.g., you might abuse your own children.

Break the Cycle of Abuse

We know that abuse victims are more likely to go on to abuse their own children. The reasons for this are complex but probably include the fact that

- parents have learned parenting (good and bad) from their own parents,

- victims feel a sense of powerlessness that they may compensate for (inappropriately) by manipulating powerless children when they grow up,

-

- an inability to cope with the stressful behavior of their children causes them to lash out, or

- the increase in drug use associated with their victimization impairs their judgment and removes inhibitions of behavior.

Some abuse victims recognize this and do not want to take the chance of having their own children, but we don't think you need to go that far. Just learn to recognize that you may have trouble coping, that there may be times you need to get help in order to cope with the stress of parenting. Learn to take a walk or count to ten before you lash out in anger and hurt your child.

Take Charge of Your Recovery from Traumatic Stress

Talking with the right people can also help. This is the T in the START-NOW program. You need to find the right people and the right time to do this, however. You can see a complete list of resources and numbers to call if you are having trauma related problems in Appendix B of this book.

Research has shown that when traumatized people talk to the wrong people at the wrong time, it makes them worse.

How do you recognize if you are talking to the wrong person? If they say things like:

- "Just forget about it."

- "You'll get over it."

- "Snap out of it."

- "If you weren't so stupid to do the things you did, you wouldn't have these problems."

- "Stop talking about that, you're upsetting your mother."

- "You shouldn't have been in that place."

- "It's your fault."

These are all negative social responses that our research has shown lead to bad outcomes. This can come from anyone, including a spouse, family member, or other person close to you. Their responses may cause additional pain, particularly if they had some perceived role in the trauma.

Good social support comes from someone who listens in an empathic and non-judgmental way, who lets you express your feelings without offering harmful advice or trying to shut you up, who validates your thoughts and feelings.

If you cannot find good social support, it is better to find someone else, or not talk at all. Individuals who have been traumatized by their own family (e.g. abuse survivors) may not be able to look to the family for useful support.

If you were abused in childhood by your father, and you look to your mother for support, you may be disappointed by your mother's complicity or denial, and that may make you feel worse. Even if at some point in time talking about the trauma to family and friends may make you feel better, there are natural time points in the recovery process when it is best for these individuals to put the idea of talking to the family out of their minds.

Sometimes when you talk about your trauma to family and friends, they don't understand, or don't appreciate what you are going through, and that can make you feel worse. It may be that at first you should focus on talking about your trauma with a professional, and talk about how you feel and how you are coping with friends and family later (if your professional is supportive to you in that).

Other things can help you in your process of recovery:

- Volunteering can be a great way to break out of a victimization cycle. This is the A is for Altruism in the START-NOW program. Were you neglected as a child? Volunteer to be a Big Brother, and help someone out who is in the same powerless position that you were in when you were younger.

- Avoid dangerous situations in high crime neighborhoods. Move, if you need to.

- Find hobbies that distract you or ways to express you feelings or your trauma. We have found that writing journals, and trying to go back to piece together the past, and put it into a realistic focus with all of the skills and experience you have as an adult (replacing the incomplete thoughts of a child) can be very helpful. This is the R in re-write you history.

Don't Isolate Yourself

Try to avoid isolating yourself. This may be needed temporarily, but sooner or later we all need contact with others.

Get your anger under control. You are right—bad things happened to you, and you have a right to be upset about it, but get upset at the people who deserve it. Don't take it out on your spouse or kids, or your co-workers, people who were never around when the bad stuff went down. They aren't to blame for that, and they shouldn't get the brunt of your anger. Anger will drive people away from you and out of your life.

Exercise, as we describe in the Better Lifestyles chapter (Chapter 12). It will help you physically and emotionally, and is a great way to let off stress. It helps you feel in control. If you look better, you will also feel better about yourself.

Get Treatment with a Professional When Needed

Beyond these self-help techniques, treatment with a professional is often useful.

Psychiatrists or your general doctor can prescribe medication. Psychiatrists, psychologists or social workers can provide psychotherapy. Counselors or pastors can provide supportive treatments and teach you ways to cope.

Your pastor or other representative of your religious faith can give you spiritual guidance. They also have a lot of experience talking to traumatized people.

The two types of treatment that have been shown to have some usefulness are medication treatment and psychotherapies. We will discuss this more later.

Treatment always begins with a thorough evaluation. The first step is to establish the diagnosis. This involves asking questions about symptoms, like depression, PTSD, substance abuse and dissociation. Participating in research studies can be a good idea, because even if you get the placebo (sugar pill), you get assessment by trauma experts, and it can be a great education.

In research studies, you are evaluated with an interview like the Structured Clinical Interview for DSM-IV that provides accurate and accepted diagnoses based on your responses to specific written questions. In PTSD studies you are often evaluated every two to four weeks with the Clinician Administered PTSD Scale (CAPS) or a similar measure. This asks specific questions about all of your PTSD symptoms, and is a great way to see what your symptoms are and how they are affected by the daily events of your life.

You may undergo an assessment of your life traumas with something like the Early Trauma Inventory, so that you have a better understanding of what is traumatic from an objective standpoint:

- Depression is measured with the Hamilton Depression Scale or Beck Depression Inventory (BDI).

- Dissociation can be measured with a variety of instruments.

- Anxiety is measured with the Hamilton Anxiety Scale.

These measures provide a way to quantitate your symptoms and see how they change with treatment.

Another important step before treatment is started is to evaluate all of your current life circumstances. If you are living in a house with an abusive spouse or boyfriend, there is no point in starting treatment before that is addressed. Most clinicians will insist that you get established in a shelter for battered persons before anything else is done.

If your children are at risk because they are being sexually abused by your partner, you need to address that. The law requires that you report child abuse to the Department of Child and Youth Services (usually a State office), the appropriate authority.

If your partner says they won't do it again, don't buy it. You will regret not taking action as soon as possible. It is in the best interest of your children. They may be taken away from you temporarily, but in the long run things will work out.

Use the time to get yourself together.

Get Your Alcohol and Substance Abuse Under Control

If you are actively abusing alcohol and other substances, you will need to address this before any trauma treatment can begin. Trauma treatment involves a reprocessing and reconstruction of traumatic memories that lead to feelings of fear and anxiety. This is not possible if the parts of the brain involved in memory are under the influence of drugs and alcohol. The brain has to be completely cleaned out before the healing process can begin. That means you will have to go through a detoxification program.

We think that twelve-step programs like Alcoholics Anonymous are great. They're free, and they have the best track record for maintaining abstinence. There are some programs that combine substance abuse and trauma treatment, focusing on trauma triggers for substance abuse, but those are not widespread. However, they are useful in our opinion.

Your initial evaluation will also involve an assessment of your level of suicidality. If you are suicidal, you cannot start treatment. Your treatment may involve a discussion of your traumatic events that may make you feel worse and that may increase your trauma-related symptoms, leading you to attempt suicide. No one who is working with you wants that to happen. You may have to be hospitalized for your suicidal thoughts.

But take heart, because of managed care, the time you spend in the hospital will be much shorter than it would have been twenty years ago.

If you are having panic attacks or you are becoming disorganized in your thinking when you think about your traumatic event that will have to be addressed.

Psychotherapy for Psychological Trauma

Psychotherapy involves talking about your traumatic events and changing your negative cognitions, as well as decreasing your levels of arousal and anxiety when you think about the event. If you have a panic attack or your mind becomes completely disorganized when you think about the event, then the treatment will not be effective.

However, your clinician will not give up on you and will continue to work with you to help you get to where you need to be. It may be that you need some treatment with medication to help you get your thoughts together before you are ready to talk about your trauma.

Trauma affects a wide range of people and can take a variety of forms. It is important to consider the context in which it occurs when thinking about treatments for trauma. When we approach a patient with psychological trauma, we consider all aspects of the context in which his or her trauma occurred.

Effects of Trauma on Psychological Development in Childhood

One of the things we consider when evaluating trauma patients is the phase of development when the person first experience psychological trauma, and whether it continued into later phases of development.

This is important because early childhood is a significant time for the development of identity, and trauma can have a profound effect on the psychological development of children.

Stressful events or disruptions in the maternal–infant bond can lead to problems with the development of a stable and secure self-identity. For these reasons, trauma that occurs early in life leads to more problems with identity as the child matures. This can contribute to identity confusion in adulthood, and, at its most extreme, personality disorders and dissociative identity disorder.

Patients with early trauma also develop multifactorial psychiatric disorders, which can include depression, somatic disorders, and alcohol and substance abuse, the trauma spectrum disorders outlined in *Does Stress Damage the Brain?* It is important to identify all of the disorders from which a trauma patient is suffering and to identify treatments for all aspects of those disorders.

Patients without a history of childhood trauma who are traumatized in adulthood — whether from a car accident, natural disaster, or events akin to those of September 11 — look similar, regardless of the trauma type. These patients typically have a more "pure" presentation of PTSD symptoms, with increased arousal and vigilance, but fewer of the depression and personality symptoms that early trauma patients develop.

These adult trauma patients respond well to cognitive behavioral therapies that concentrate on processing of the actual traumatic event, with a desensitization to aspects of the event that increase arousal and intrusive memories. With time, the traumatic event is processed both emotionally and cognitively, and negative cognitions and other unhelpful cognitive processes are corrected — the event is placed in a proper context and integrated into the patient's catalogue of life experiences.

These patients can also benefit from medication treatment in conjunction with behavioral treatments, such as SSRIs (Selective Serotonin Reuptake Inhibitors).

Early trauma patients, on the other hand, have a more complicated presentation and do not always benefit from traditional cognitive behavioral therapies. For these patients, the reintroduction of traumatic memories may be associated with an increase in dissociation, negative emotions, or identity confusions and crises that the patient cannot control. In such situations, retrieving traumatic memories for attempted therapeutic benefit is not always helpful.

Some early trauma patients need long-term therapies aimed at psychological support, supplemented with medications where appropriate. Many early trauma patients who have disabling psychiatric symptoms are treated with multiple medications, which may include SSRI and a mood-stabilizing agent like valproic acid (Valproate) or carbamazepine (Tegretol).

Although patients who have their first traumatic event in adulthood look very similar in terms of their symptoms, regardless of trauma type, there are some aspects of trauma that influence what kinds of symptoms you might have. This is largely related to different trauma types leading to different types of fear reactions. For example, women who are victims of sexual assault will be more likely to have problems with sexual intimacy, related to fear responses associated to sexual activity. Conversely, motor vehicle accident victims may have fear responses related to approaching an automobile.

The Meaning of Psychological Trauma

The response to trauma is also influenced by factors such as the meaning the event had for the individual, and social and cultural factors related to the event.

Children who are sexually abused by a biological parent whom they trust and rely on for caregiving and support will have a different response than someone who is victimized by a stranger. Also, patients who are not able to talk about their trauma in a supportive environment and social context may have additional suffering.

Many veterans of the Vietnam War, upon returning to the United States, did not find their country to be supportive of the sacrifices they made. Similarly, in Muslim countries there is great shame for women to admit they have been victims of sexual assault. Therefore, in countries such as Bosnia where there was systematic rape of the female population, many families do not want to talk about their traumatic experiences.

The Neuroscience of Early Interventions for Trauma

Appropriate treatment of trauma victims may require rapid interventions soon after the trauma.

We know from animal studies that memories are not immediately engraved in the mind—it can take a month or more before they become indelible. For instance, animals that undergo lesions of the hippocampus within the first month after an aversive memory lose all recall of what happened.

During this time period, the memories continue to be susceptible to modification; this time period is known as memory consolidation. However, if you wait too long, a month or more, it is no longer possible to erase the negative memory simply by lesioning the hippocampus. At that point, the memory becomes engraved in the long-term memory storage areas in the cerebral cortex, the outermost part of the brain.

After the memory has become engraved in long-term memory storage, it is indelible and no longer easily amenable to modification. This may represent the case of, for example, combat veterans with longstanding PTSD, for whom no amount of treatment is able to erase the traumatic memories of their combat experiences.

That is why it is important to intervene early, before the traumatic memories become indelible.

Animal studies indicate that early interventions will be beneficial before traumatic memories become firmly engraved in the mind. We know from these studies that medications given before exposure to trauma—including valium-type medications, antidepressants, opiates, and alcohol—can diminish or prevent the long-term behavioral effects of stressors.

Clinical studies also show that some medications given before a trauma can prevent long-term psychopathology. For example, in a study of people exposed to a hotel fire, those individuals who were intoxicated with alcohol at the time of the fire had a better psychiatric outcome than did those who were not. This may mean that it is better to get treatment before you are even diagnosed with having a psychiatric disorder, which often requires having symptoms for at least a month.

Get Started Now on your Path to Recovery

Now is the time to get started on the real path toward a real recovery from psychological trauma. This is a journey you will mostly take by yourself, although there are some parts that will involve loved ones, family, and friends.

One important step that we've mentioned already is the R in START, Re-write your own history. You need to re-write your memories in order to fully and finally get over the trauma. Part of that re-writing involves educating yourself about trauma in general, but part of it involves getting more details about your own experience. Sometimes this work really needs to be done with a professional, which will be discussed later; however, sometimes, you can do a lot of this work yourself or with a loved one. You'll need to go back and gather information from friends, relatives and others who are in a position to have a fuller, and often, less distorted picture of the traumatic events. You may need to physically go back to the scene of your trauma and Re-visit it so that you can re-write your history accurately.

But first, before you re-visit your trauma, you'll need to Seek Safety and Support. This is the critical "S" that is the beginning and foundation of the START program. You can begin to express your feelings about the trauma and start to share the experience with someone else. This can be a tricky business.

Talking is a good way to share, but there are also other very effective ways of sharing. For some people, expressing their feelings through art can be very helpful. For others, writing down their feelings and their experiences can be enormously liberating.

How to Identify Your Own Trauma-related Behavior

How do you tell if your behaviors are related to your trauma? There are some typical patterns of behavior that are easy to recognize, once you know what to look for. You may have already started to recognize some of these behaviors in yourself by reading this book.

The more you can make the connection between your behavior and your trauma, the better off you'll be.

Some of these behaviors include

- getting very angry for no reason,

- feeling intense anger when in the presence of someone you feel is trying to control or manipulate you

- perhaps you have to sit with your back against the wall in a restaurant

- you feel nauseous when someone wants to have sex with you

- some people feel very bad inside and have to drink or take drugs to get rid of the feeling

- if you were raped in an enclosed space, you may have trouble getting on elevators, especially if there is someone else already on it. Does your heart rate go up and you become sweaty? That may be a clue.

- if you were a soldier in Iraq where improvised explosive devices (IEDs) were hidden in bags of garbage by the side of the road, you may have anxiety reactions on your way to the grocery store seeing bags of garbage on the side of the road, even when there is no real threat. This may make you drive fast down the middle of the road, or feel like you always have to drive. Maybe you get angry when stuck behind a slow moving motorist. This just represents a learned behavior that had survival value in Iraq. The trick is to "unlearn" it when you come home.

As a trauma survivor, you need to understand your own symptoms and how to address them effectively. For example, PTSD patients have difficulty coping with minor stresses. If you suffer from PTSD, you must do everything you can to eliminate potential stressors in your daily life. A loved one can be enormously helpful in this process, as we will explain in a later chapter.

Trauma and Grief

Sometimes after psychological trauma there is a blockage of the normal grief reaction. Psychiatrists are increasingly talking about grief as evidence of a mental condition, but in fact it is a normal part of the healing process after we lose someone close to us.

A doctor named Elisabeth Kubler-Ross wrote a book in 1969 called *On Death and Dying* that remains to this day a classic guidebook on the grief process. She described five stages of grief that follow the sudden loss of a loved one, like a spouse, parent, close friend, or child:

- The first stage is denial. You are in a state of shock. You say there must have been a mistake, or maybe I heard it wrong. Maybe someone is playing a joke. I just saw that person yesterday, and they looked fine.

- With time the reality sets in that the person really is gone, and then denial turns to anger. Why couldn't the doctors have done something to save their life? Why didn't someone call 911 right away? Why did the person have to do x or y, thus putting themselves at risk? Why is God so unjust?

- The next stage is bargaining, where you may try to talk to God and make a deal to bring the person back, or maybe you make a promise to change your life or do some charitable activity in exchange for the loved one coming back.

- When it becomes clear that bargaining is useless, the person who was left behind succumbs to depression.

- But finally, maybe weeks or months later, arrives acceptance of the loss, and the realization that this is just

FIGURE 11: STAGES OF GRIEF

part of life, no matter how unfair it seems.

Another theory for grief that many people have found helpful is J. William Worden's book, *Grief Counseling and Grief Therapy: A Handbook for the Mental Health Practitioner.* Worden's approach is proactive.

Worden recommends four tasks to complete the process of mourning. Just like our START NOW program, he thinks that the path to recovery is more of a circle than a straight line. You may need to come back to some points of the process and do them again. Another thing is that you can't put your grief work on a schedule. Everyone's different and there are so many things involved that you may think you are done but then you get surprised by how it seems like your grief is circling back again and starting all over. Don't panic — this is the way the grief process works.

The First Task: The first task Worden identifies is "To accept the reality of the loss" which includes not just the fact of the loss but also the significance of the loss. Simple things like going to a funeral or talking (and thinking) about the person in the past tense help us accept the reality of the loss. Even though you talk about someone in the past tense, however, it may not hit right away how significant the loss really is. For instance, people might downplay how important that person was to them, which is a way of denying the impact the loss has had or will have on them.

Often a big hurdle to overcome in the grieving process is coming to terms with how the person died. If someone kills themselves it is common for people to feel like that person didn't want to be with them anymore. Not only do you have to mourn the loss of your loved one, you also have to come to terms with what the suicide means to you personally. Death by drug or alcohol overdose is similar in that it is a self-inflicted death, and may have a stigma that makes it hard to be open and talk about your feelings. Maybe your loved one died in a foreign combat zone, or maybe they disappeared and their body was never found. What happens to the body is very important. The ancient Greeks fought whole battles over trying to get the bodies of their dead soldiers back from their enemies!

The Second Task: The second task is "To work through the pain of grief". Each person will experience a range of different emotions after someone dies. None of these feelings are abnormal or wrong, although some may be more difficult to resolve. Sadness, fear, loneliness, despair, hopelessness, anger, guilt, blame, shame and even relief are all emotions you might have to contend with. As we will be going over later the "T" in START Now is for Talking about your feelings, which makes you realize that they are real. Here in the USA we don't do a very good job of dealing with death, and a lot of people don't feel comfortable talking about it or feel like they might say the wrong thing. They might think that if they just ignore the fact that someone died the uncomfortableness will just go away. It is never a good idea, though, to deny or avoid our feelings about the death of a loved one. A simple but good thing to say is "I'm sorry for your loss." Or maybe you can add "I'll be thinking about you." That is not patronizing but it expresses that you care and acknowledges to the person the importance of what happened. Reach out and find the positive support you need to talk about your feelings (as you will learn later, "S" is for Seek Safety and Support). You can also take

Action or practice Altruism (the "A" in, guess what?) like setting up a scholarship or memorial in honor of the person you lost..

The Third Task: Task three is "To adjust to an environment in which the deceased is missing". It can take a long time to get used to the person not being around, not only with your feelings, but things like not having another person in the house, or having to learn how to do the finances if that person always took care of that..

The Fourth Task: Finally, task four is "To find an enduring connection with the deceased while embarking on a new life". Worden recognized that people need to continue to feel connected with the person who died. He would never say, "Just snap out of it". You can tell how far along you are on this task by observing how difficult or easy it is to have thoughts and memories of the person who died.

When someone dies you might feel like your life has stopped or that you will never be able to feel joy or pleasure again. Don't worry, this is a normal reaction, and it may take a long time to go away. Again, don't put a time schedule on it. However, if you follow the points in this book, you will one day again be able to enjoy things. Trust us!

It is important that you allow yourself to express your feelings, including sorrow and sadness. If you don't, you will never regain the emotional equilibrium that allows you to feel extreme joy. Numbing out the grief has a way of taking out all feelings with it. Remember, only you can feel your feelings. Don't let other people tell you how you feel. And most importantly of all, don't listen to people who tell you to "just get over it."

Many times victims of psychological trauma get stuck in the grieving process. They are so overwhelmed by the tragedy that they can't move through the normal grieving process. Or maybe they are in dangerous circumstances, like a war zone, and don't have the opportunity to grieve. Children who are in an abusive family are not encouraged to express their feelings.

Many of the combat veterans with PTSD I have treated over the years describe a feeling of numbness when someone in their family dies. As one vet told me, "they have to get in line to be grieved for, because I have a whole string of people I never grieved for who died in Vietnam."

In my own circumstance, I did not grieve for the loss of my mother when I was four years old, and it caught up with me forty years later. As I describe in my book, *The Goose That Laid the Golden Egg*, I had to learn to grieve as an adult, and let myself go through the process. It took about a year, and wasn't always easy, but I am glad I did it, because I believe it enhanced my ability to feel deep emotions...and to empathize with others who need to go through this process, too.

These are just some of the things survivors can do to help themselves move towards recovery. We will talk more about what you can do to get on the road to real recovery from traumatic stress when we outline the START-NOW program in detail in later chapters. But first, we will talk about currently established conventional treatments involving psychotherapy and medications that can serve a complementary role for everything else you are doing to get back on the road to recovery.

The reality is that it might take you up to a year to recover from devastating loss, as described in the book *Healing After Loss, Daily Meditations for Recovery from Grief*, by Martha Whitmore Hickman. That book has a meditation on grief and loss, sometimes with quotes from literature, for every day of the week. If you think that you have someone you haven't grieved for, we recommend that you get the book, and read each day's entry for every day of the week. It will help you get your emotions flowing.

It is important that you allow yourself to express your feelings, including sorrow and sadness. If you don't, you will never regain the emotional equilibrium that allows you to feel extreme joy. Because numbing out the grief has a way of taking out all feelings with it. Remember, only you can feel your feelings. Don't let other people tell you how you feel. And most importantly of all, don't listen to people who tell you to "just get over it."

Many times victims of psychological trauma get stuck in the grieving process. They are so overwhelmed by the tragedy that they can't move through the normal grieving process. Or maybe they are in dangerous circumstances, like a war zone, and don't have the opportunity to grieve. Children who are in an abusive family are not encouraged to express their feelings.

Many of the combat veterans with PTSD I have treated over the years describe a feeling of numbness when someone in their family dies. As one vet told me, "they have to get in line to be grieved for, because I have a whole string of people I never grieved for who died in Vietnam."

In my own circumstance, I did not grieve for the loss of my mother when I was four years old, and it caught up with me forty years later. As I describe in my book, *The Goose That Laid the Golden Egg*, I had to learn to grieve as an adult, and let myself go through the process. It took about a year, and wasn't always easy, but I am glad I did it, because I believe it enhanced my ability to feel deep emotions...and to empathize with others who need to go through this process, too.

These are just some of the things survivors can do to help themselves move towards recovery. We will talk more about what you can do to get on the road to real recovery from traumatic stress when we outline the START-NOW program in detail in later chapters. But first, we will talk about currently established conventional treatments involving psychotherapy and medications that can serve a complementary role for everything else you are doing to get back on the road to recovery.

CHAPTER 9: MEDICATIONS FOR TRAUMA-RELATED MENTAL CONDITIONS

While most people can do a lot to help themselves, especially with the tools you're learning about in this book, some people may need the boost of professional help to fully recover from their trauma. Some of the treatments we talk about in this chapter have been scientifically proven to help trauma victims.

But how do you know if you need professional treatment, and what treatments will work for you?

For some people, the first step in the recovery process may involve taking medication. That means going to your medical doctor for a prescription. Or maybe your therapist will refer you to a psychiatrist, who is the medical doctor in your mental health treatment team who has the ability and expertise to prescribe medications for mental health problems.

Problem is, most psychiatrists schedule patients in fifteen-minute visits. You may get more time for the initial visit, when s/he will do a full evaluation of your symptoms, and possibly make a diagnosis of a mental condition, but after that, insurance companies won't pay for more. We're expensive!

So that means you might leave with a prescription for a pill, but not with your questions answered because there wasn't enough time, or there was too much going on and you didn't think of all the questions you had for your MD or psychiatrist. The next time you come back, you've only got fifteen minutes. Your head is swimming with all the terms and the names of the medications: antidepressants, antipsychotics, benzodiazepines...it goes on and on.

And the names! Abilify, trazodone; each drug has at least two names, one the "generic" name and the other the "brand" name given by the drug company that made it. They actually make the generic names hard to remember so you're more like to remember the brand. How can you remember all those names? The fact is, you can't. I've been prescribing them for years, and I still have to Google them sometimes to remember how to spell them.

So what's a person to do?

Since doctors don't have time to explain it all to you, and since your Uncle Tom doesn't have a clue, we'll get . . . a pharmacist!

Fortunately, at our neighborhood pharmacy I know someone named Fred the Friendly Pharmacist, who will give us a personal tour of his pharmacy and explain it all to you. Normally they don't let you go behind the counter, but he's going to do it just this one time as a special favor.

Here we go!

Antidepressants

Okay, the first shelf in Fred's pharmacy holds the antidepressants. As the name implies, they were developed to fight depression, but what can be a little confusing sometimes is that they also treat other mental problems, like anxiety and PTSD. Truth is, there is a lot of overlap in the symptoms of mental conditions, and it is not uncommon for drugs developed for one problem to work for another. If they were tested first on PTSD patients, they'd be called anti-PTSD drugs, but since they were tested in depression first, the name stuck, and people continue to use it.

Tricyclic Antidepressant Medications

The first group of antidepressant drugs they developed, called tricyclics, worked mainly on the adrenaline, or norepinephrine, system of the brain.

Fred keeps them right here, on the top shelf on the left. One of his pharmacy assistants named Pam is really short and needs a step ladder to get up there, but doctors don't prescribe them as often as they used to so it doesn't make much difference. Even though they need more space for the new kind of diabetes drugs that just came out and are all the rage these days, they still keep the tricyclics around because some people experience side effects from the other drugs; the tricyclics are a possible solution.

When Fred the Pharmacist gives out tricyclics, including imipramine and amitriptyline, he always tells people to watch out for side effects that might affect another part of the nervous system called the cholinergic nervous system. He does this because he knows the pills can be helpful if people stay on them for at least a couple of weeks, and these side effects are usually not dangerous and go away before then. Fred feels that if patients are made aware of what to expect, they can become more effective partners in their mental health care.

The side effects that Fred always makes sure to warn people about are:

- dry mouth,

- problems urinating,

- blurred vision,

- decreased bowel function, and;

- possibly effects on heart function.

Although Fred knows these side effects are no big deal, he also knows that some people get a little freaky when they hear about them. Also, when newer antidepressants came on the market, the drug salesmen convinced people to move to their new brands, so even though the old ones may work just as well for depression, they aren't used as much anymore.

Antidepressant Medications With Other Mechanisms of Action

We know, we know. This is quite a mouthful, but that's the way Fred thinks of all those antidepressant drugs that came after the tricyclics, and before the current crop of drugs (the serotonin reuptake inhibitors (SSRI) that we will get to next and that work on the—you guessed it—the serotonin system.)

These drugs, which Fred keeps on a shelf right below the tricyclics, work on other brain chemical systems besides norepinephrine and serotonin, such as dopamine. Fred likes to think of dopamine as the "happy" brain chemical, since taking medications like bupropion (Wellbutrin) increase the levels of dopamine in your system and make you, well, happier. Fred, being a happy kind of guy himself, likes helping other people get happier.

He also likes people to be healthy (happy and healthy, got it?) so he always tries to help people quit smoking, for which he has bupropion sold under another brand name (Zyban) just for that purpose. That way the docs can tell people they're getting an anti-smoking drug (i.e., not an antidepressant, which might freak them out) even though it is identical to Wellbutrin. Side effects include:

- weight loss

- restlessness

- rarely, at high doses, seizures

The other antidepressant medications on Fred's "happy" shelf, as he likes to call it, also work on dopamine and/or do not have specific actions on norepinephrine or serotonin. These include

- trazodone (Desyrel)

- maprotaline (Ludiomil)

- mirtazapine (Remeron)

Like Wellbutrin, these drugs don't have as many anticholinergic side effects and effects on the heart and blood pressure. They also don't have as many sexual side effects as the SSRIs (see below). Desyrel can rarely cause priapism (extended painful erection that requires emergency treatment). It is often used to treat insomnia in patients with PTSD and depression. Side effects of Remeron include:

- sweating

- tiredness

- strange dreams

- elevation of lipids

- weight gain

- upset stomach

- anxiety

- agitation

Selective Serotonin Reuptake Inhibitors (SSRIs)

This brings us to the last group of antidepressant medications which Fred keeps on his lower left shelf where they can be grabbed easily. They are (ta-dum!) the selective serotonin reuptake inhibitors (SSRIs).

These drugs boost serotonin levels in the brain by blocking the ability of brain cells to take back or do "reuptake" of serotonin in the space between the brain cells, therefore effectively "increasing" serotonin levels in the brain.

SSRIs include:

- paroxetine (Paxil)

- fluoxetine (Prozac)

- sertraline (Zoloft)

- fluvoxamine (Luvox)

- citalopram (Celexa)

- escitalopram (Lexapro)

Paroxetine and sertraline are approved for the treatment of PTSD by the FDA. All of them are approved for the treatment of depression.

Fred ALWAYS makes sure to warn people about a loss of libido or other sexual side effects because he knows that people are too shy to tell their doctors unless they know the sexual side effects can come from the drug. The SSRIs have fewer anti-cholinergic side effects than the tricyclics. Side effects can include:

- nausea,

- diarrhea,

- headache,

- insomnia, and;

- agitation

If you suddenly stop taking your SSRIs, you can feel suicidal, so Fred says don't do it. Your physician will tell you how to stop taking them.

Dual Reuptake Inhibitors (SNRIs)

Recently Fred had to push the SSRIs over to the left side of his lowest shelf to make room for a new group of antidepressants that work to boost both the serotonin and norepinephrine systems. These drugs are called (yep), serotonin and norepinephrine reuptake inhibitors (SNRIs), and include venlafaxine (Effexor) and duloxetine (Cymbalta).

In general, venlafaxine and duloxetine seem to work better for depression than SSRIs and tricyclics, but they also increase the risk for suicidal thoughts compared to the SSRIs and tricyclics, although these occur rarely (isn't it weird that a drug for the treatment of depression and suicide might make you more, um, suicidal?).

When a number of studies were looked at together, overall, venlafaxine had a success rate of 74% — that's statistically significantly better than SSRIs, which only have a 61% success rate, and tricyclics, which only have a 58% success rate.

As you can see, tricyclics work just as well for depression as the SSRIs but more people who were taking tricyclics stopped taking their medication because of side effects than people on SSRIs.

Fred is careful to inform his patients that both venlafaxine and duloxetine can cause

- dizziness, constipation, dry mouth, headache, changes in sleep, or

- more rarely a serotonin syndrome, with restlessness, shivering and sweating.

- A decrease in saliva can cause cavities.

- Venlafaxine has been associated with a dose dependent increase in blood pressure.

- Venlafaxine seems to carry the greatest risk of suicidality amongst all of the antidepressants, with three-fold increased risk of attempted or completed suicides.

Antidepressant and Mood Stabilizer Medications: Use and Risks

Drug	Use	Common, benign side effects	Serious side effects	Life threatening side effects	Reasons not to take
TRICYCLICS Moderate Risk					
doxepin (Sinequaan) or imipramine (Tofranil)	Major depression	Dry mouth, constipation, memory, blurred vision, urination, sexual function	Blood pressure changes,	Heart arrhythmias, overdose	Heart condition
amitriptyline (Elavil) or amoxapine (Asendin)	Major depression	Dry mouth, constipation, memory, blurred	Blood pressure changes,	Heart arrhythmias, overdose	Heart condition, seizures, glaucoma

Drug	Use	Common, benign side effects	Serious side effects	Life threatening side effects	Reasons not to take
		vision, urination, sexual function			
Norepinephrine Reuptake Inhibitors *Low Risk*					
desipramine (Norpramin) *or* nortriptyline (Aventyl, Pamelor) *or* amoxapine (Ascendin)	Major depression	Dry mouth, constipation, memory	blurred vision, urination, sexual function	Heart arrhythmias, seizures	Heart condition, seizures, glaucoma
clomipramine (Anafranil)	OCD	Dry mouth, constipation, memory	blurred vision, urination, sexual function	Heart arrhythmias, seizures	Heart condition, seizures, glaucoma
MAO Inhibitors *Moderate Risk*					
phenalzine (Nardil) *or* tranylcypromine (Parnate)	Major depression	constipation, blurred vision, urination, sexual function	Dizziness, headache, insomnia	Wine and cheese hypertensive crisis, liver damage, anemia	Liver disease, heart failure, pheochromocytoma, children
Quatrocyclics *Low Risk*					
mirtazapine (Remeron)	Major depression	Shivering, fatigue, nightmares, weight	Lipid elevations,	Trouble breathing, sore throat	Kidney or liver disease, MAOI

Drug	Use	Common, benign side effects	Serious side effects	Life threatening side effects	Reasons not to take
		gain, anxiety, dry mouth, constipation	swelling, muscle pain		
maprotiline (Ludiomil)	Major depression	Dry mouth, drowsiness, nausea, vomiting	Rash, swelling	Seizures, hallucinations, irregular heart rate, jaundice	Liver disease, MAOI
Selective Serotonin Reuptake Inhibitors (SSRI) *Low Risk*					
paroxetine (Paxil)	Major depression, panic, OCD, PTSD, GAD	Nausea, diarrhea, headache, insomnia	Decreased libido, akithisia	Suicidal thoughts, mood swings with dose change	Allergic reaction, MAOI
sertraline (Zoloft)	Major depression, panic, OCD, PTSD, GAD	Nausea, diarrhea, headache, insomnia	Decreased libido, akithisia	uicidal thoughts, mood swings with dose change, bleeding	Allergic reaction, MAOI
fluoxetine (Prozac)	Major depression and OCD	Nausea, diarrhea, headache, insomnia	Decreased libido, akithisia	Suicidal thoughts, mood swings with dose chang	Allergic reaction, MAOI
fluvoxamine (Luvox)	Major depression	Nausea, diarrhea, headache,	Decreased libido, akithisia	Suicidal thoughts, mood	Allergic reaction, MAOI

Drug	Use	Common, benign side effects	Serious side effects	Life threatening side effects	Reasons not to take
		insomnia		swings with dose change	
Other Antidepressants					
bupropion (Wellbutrin, Zyban)	Depression, smoking cessation	Weight loss, restlessness, dry mouth, insomnia, con-stipation, nausea, vomiting		Seizures	Seizure disorder, allergic to medication
trazodone (Desyrel)	Major depression	Dizziness, constipation, dry mouth, headache	Priapism	Allergic reaction, irregular heart rate	Allergy to medication, pregnancy, acute heart disease
Dual Uptake Inhibitors					
venlafaxine (Effexor)	Major depression	Restlessness, shivering, constipation, nausea, headache	Sexual dysfunction, hypertension, muscle cramp	Suicidality, stomach bleeding, allergic reaction	Allergy to drug, MAOI
duloxetine (Cymbalta)	Major depression	Constipation, nausea, diarrhea, vomiting, dry mouth	Sexual dysfunction, blurred vision, muscle pain, dizziness	Stomach bleeding, liver damage	Allergy to drug, MAOI
Mood stabilizers					

Drug	Use	Common, benign side effects	Serious side effects	Life threatening side effects	Reasons not to take
lithium (Lithobid)	Bipolar disorder	Nausea, tremor, weight gain, diarrhea, thirst	Blurred vision, stomach upset	Change in renal function	Heart disease, renal disease, brain damage, diuretics
valproic acid (Valproate, Depakene, Depakote)	Bipolar disorder	Mood change, anorexia, nausea, trembling	Rash, dizziness	Liver failure, birth defects, bleeding, pancreatitis	Liver disease, pregnancy, breast feeding
carbamazepine (Tegretol)	Bipolar disorder	Dizziness, drowsiness, nausea, vomiting	Confusion, depression, hallucinations	Bone marrow suppression, heart failure, liver dysfunction	Hypersensitivity, pregnancy, breast feeding, Allergy to medication
topiramate (Topomax)	Bipolar disorder	Dizziness, nervousness, headache, irritability	Confusion, aggression	Low blood sugar, blurred vision	Allergy to medication
lamotrigine (Lamictal)	Bipolar disorder	Dizziness, headache, sleepiness, nausea, vomiting	Blurred vision,	Steven Johnson syndrome	Allergy to medication
gabapentin (Neurontin)	Bipolar disorder	Dizziness, headache, sleepiness, nausea, vomiting	Blurred vision	Eye movements	Allergy to medication

FIGURE 12: ANTIDEPRESSANTS AND MOOD STABILIZERS: USES AND MAJOR RISKS

All medication tables are adapted from BEFORE YOU TAKE THAT PILL, by J. Douglas Bremner, © 2008 J.

Douglas Bremner, used by permission of Avery Publishing,
an imprint of the Penguin Group (see Appendix D).

We first met Fred after he read in a magazine about our research on the effects of antidepressant medications on the brain in patients with PTSD or depression related to psychological trauma. Being a curious guy, he sent us an email asking for more information.

We told him that antidepressant drugs have been shown in animal studies to have effects on parts of the brain involved in the stress response. Studies in animals found that SSRIs increase branching and growth of brain cells, or neurons, in the hippocampus, which as mentioned previously, is a brain area that plays a critical role in learning and memory, and it's very sensitive to stress.

Fred was interested to learn that treatment with the SSRI paroxetine (Paxil) in PTSD patients for a year resulted in a 5% increase in hippocampal volume measured with magnetic resonance imaging (MRI) and a 35% improvement in hippocampal-based memory function (for example, the ability to remember a paragraph or a list of words) as measured with neuropsychological testing. These patients felt that treatment with paroxetine led to a significant improvement in their ability to work and function in their lives. They were able to concentrate and remember things much better than before treatment with medication.

The Story of Jeff, with PTSD

One of the patients who was treated with paroxetine in one of our studies was a man named Jeff. Here's his story:

Jeff had been a cop in the Bridgeport, Connecticut, police force for twenty years. When he entered our study, he had reached a crisis point where he couldn't cope with his daily memories of a traumatic event that happened fifteen years before. His wife told him he should get counseling right away.

The morning of the incident, he took a call at 5 a.m. concerning a suicide attempt. It was only four blocks away.

When he entered the house, a woman was screaming, "My son hurt himself, he didn't mean it, you've got to help him."

The father was very silent.

A five-year-old girl was crying and saying, "Help my brother, he's hurt."

Jeff entered the room. What had been a seventeen-year-old boy was lying on his bed with a shotgun on his chest. His face looked normal, but the top of his head was a cavity. He had literally blown his brains out. The boy's body was making a gasping sound as if he were breathing. As Jeff stood there, some of the brains sticking to the ceiling fell on his shoulder.

Following this incident, Jeff was bothered daily by memories of the event. He said, "I drift from one thing to another. Nothing seems to have any meaning anymore. I feel as if my life will end tomorrow, but I don't care."

Jeff would think over and over about how this thing happened, how it could have been prevented. The boy was depressed because he had acne, and thought a girl he liked wouldn't like him in turn. Jeff would ponder about how this could be his own son. He was tormented by his thoughts.

Sometimes, when he was reliving the event, he wasn't aware of anything around him. He tried to talk about it, he tried to be a tough cop and hold it in, but nothing relieved his anguish.

We started Jeff on Paxil at a variable dose. Within six weeks, Jeff showed an improvement in a number of PTSD symptoms, including intrusive symptoms like recurrent mental images of his trauma. He appeared to have an almost complete resolution of the symptoms that were causing him so much distress.

Other Medications for Treatment of Psychological Trauma

Fred the friendly pharmacist says that he has seen doctors prescribe other drugs for the treatment of PTSD and depression. When he first saw these other drugs used this way, he scratched his head, since they weren't approved for these problems by the Food and Drug Administration (FDA).

But since he's a clever, competent and curious kind of guy, he went to the library at his pharmacy school and looked up some articles on the use of these medications for these problems. Fred is happy to talk with you about the details of the research studies in the articles, but since he knows you are eager to get your medications and go home and read more about tools for recovery from psychological trauma, he's going to tell you there's good reason to think that the following medications might be useful for PTSD and depression:

- The antihypertension drug, prazosin (Minipres), has been shown in research studies to improve both symptoms of PTSD as well as nightmares and insomnia.

- We have had good results with the epilepsy drug, phenytoin (Dilantin), which has also been shown to block the effects of stress on the brain in animal studies, and which we have shown to increase brain volumes in PTSD patients.

- Some studies have shown that the beta blocker drug, propranolol, used to treat hypertension, can prevent the development of chronic PTSD when given soon after the trauma.

While medication may be a good start in itself, it's usually not enough, which is what the rest of this book is about. And Fred agrees. After all, he doesn't care if you take prescription medications. He just wants you to feel better.

You can read more about medication treatment of PTSD and depression in *Before You Take That Pill: Why the Drug Industry May Be Bad For Your Health*, published by Penguin in 2008.

Antipsychotic Medication

Fred has a number of patients with schizophrenia who have been coming to him for years to get their prescriptions filled for antipsychotic medications. The second shelf in his pharmacy, to the right of the antidepressants, is reserved for the antipsychotics (also known as neuroleptics). Although Fred worries about people taking these drugs since they can cause weight gain, diabetes, and tardive dyskinesia (a twitching in the face or other areas), he's seen some of these people when they stop taking their medications so he always encourages them to stay with it. Over the years, though, Fred has seen more and more people getting antipsychotics who don't have schizophrenia. A lot of these people have PTSD or depression related to psychological trauma.

Fred knows that many psychiatrists will prescribe anti-psychotics for patients with depression who do not respond to antidepressants. That's because some studies show that the addition of antipsychotics leads to a small but statistically significant improvement in depression, although for every person who gets better, one develops the disturbing symptom of akathisia (a feeling like you want to jump out of your skin). Fortunately, this symptom goes away when you stop the drug.

You may have seen advertisements on television for antipsychotic drugs like Abilify (aripiprazole) used in the treatment of depression. They show happy people floating out to their mailboxes, followed by an announcer reading a huge list of possible side effects as fast as he can (and the volume decreases dramatically.)

The top shelf in Fred's second row of shelves is reserved for the original group of antipsychotic medications, the typical antipsychotics, the first in that class being chlorpromazine (Thorazine). Its discovery half a century ago led to a miraculous clearing out of the mental hospitals housing tons of people with previously untreatable schizophrenia.

The typical antipsychotic medications block the dopamine 2 receptor in the brain, which is involved in the symptoms of psychosis. Other first generation antipsychotics include thioridazine (Mellaril), perphenazine (Trilafon), fluphenazine (Prolixin), haloperidol (Haldol), loxapine (Loxatane), and thiothixene (Navane).

Fred tells his patients that the typical antipsychotics can be associated with some pretty troubling side effects that are worse than with the antidepressants:

- extra-pyramidal side effects (involuntary muscle movements), including Parkinsonism, with tremor, rigidity, and shuffling gait;

- patients also develop akathisia, a feeling of internal stiffness or restlessness that can be very uncomfortable, or dyskinesia, a painful stiffening of the muscles.

- a more long-term troubling possible side effect is Tardive Dyskinesia, which involves twitching, jerking movements, and lip smacking, of the lips, mouth, and arms.

- antipsychotics can also cause anti-cholinergic side effects (confusion, memory problems, dry mouth), sedation, and a lowering of the blood pressure.

The second shelf in Fred's pharmacy just below the typical antipsychotic are the newer group of atypical antipsychotics, which block a range of different dopamine receptors as well as other receptors like the serotonin 2A receptors. It is thought that this is the reason they are not associated as often with extra pyramidal side effects as commonly.

Atypical antipsychotic drugs include olanzapine (Zyprexa), risperidone (Risperdal), ziprasidone (Geodon), quetiapine (Seroquel), and aripiprazole (Abilify). These medications have not, however, been clearly been shown to work better than the typical antipsychotics. Side effects of atypical antipsychotics include

- drowsiness,

- drops in blood pressure,

- weight gain, and

- decreased sweating which may increase the risk of heat stroke.

Fred worries most about the possibility that the newer atypical antipsychotics can interfere with glucose (sugar) metabolism, which increases the risk of weight gain and diabetes.

Antipsychotic Medications: Uses and Risks

Drug	Indication	Common, benign side effects	Serious side effects	Life threatening side effects	Reasons not to take
Typical Antipsychotics *Medium Risk*					
chlorpromazine (Thorazine) *or* fluphenazine (Prolixin) *or* haloperidol (Haldol) *or* loxapine (Loxatane) *or* thioridazine (Mellaril) *or* thiothixene (Navane)	Schizophrenia	Confusion, dry mouth, memory problems, sedation	Parkinsonism, tremor, rigidity, akithisia, dyskinesia, tardive dyskinesia	Orthostatic hypotension, neuroleptic malignant syndrome	Hypersensitivity
mesoridazine (Serentil) *or* perphenazine (Trilafon)	Schizophrenia	Confusion, dry mouth, memory problems, sedation	Parkinsonism, tremor, rigidity, akithisia, dyskinesia, tardive dyskinesia	Orthostatic hypotension, neuroleptic malignant syndrome Prolongation of QT interval with cardiac death	Prolonged QT interval or heart disease; hypersensitivity
Atypical Antipsychotics *Medium Risk*					
olanzepine	Schizophren	Drowsines	Weight	Neuroleptic	Hypersensitivi

Drug	Indication	Common, benign side effects	Serious side effects	Life threatening side effects	Reasons not to take
(Zyprexa) or risperidone (Risperdal)	ia	s, decreased sweating, headache, nausea, vomiting	gain, constipation	malignant syndrome, diabetes	ty
ziprasidone (Geodon)	Schizophrenia	Drowsiness, decreased sweating, headache, nausea, vomiting	Weight gain, constipation	Neuroleptic malignant syndrome Increases QT interval with risk of cardiac death	Hypersensitivity
quetiapine (Seroquel) or aripiprazole (Abilify)	Schizophrenia	Drowsiness, decreased sweating, headache, nausea, vomiting	Weight gain, constipation	Neuroleptic malignant syndrome	Hypersensitivity
Atypical Antipsychotics *High Risk*					
clozapine (Clozaril)	Schizophrenia	Drowsiness, decreased sweating, headache, nausea, vomiting	Weight gain, constipation	Agranulocyto-sis (1%), seizures, myocarditis, lowering of pressure, Neuroleptic malignant syndrome, diabetes	Hypersensitivity

FIGURE 13: ANTIPSYCHOTIC MEDICATIONS: USES & RISKS

Medications for the Treatment of Insomnia

Fred's pharmacy is open twenty-four hours a day, and some of
his colleagues on the night shift have told him about bleary-eyed
people who come in the middle of the night holding prescriptions for
sleep medications in their hands, and that more and more people
have trouble sleeping. In fact, one out of four Americans now has a
sleep problem. Fred always tells these people that sleeping pills (anti-
insomnia medications) may be helpful for short-term problems, but
they may need other non-medication treatments for insomnia in the
long run.

People with a history of psychological trauma, especially those
with PTSD or depression, have more trouble sleeping at night than
most folks. They are often prescribed sleep medications by their
doctors.

Insomnia can lead to a host of other problems. For instance, about
40% of people with insomnia also suffer from anxiety or depression. It
is difficult to say whether the insomnia or the mental disorder comes
first. Trouble falling and staying asleep can also affect memory and
cognition (thought processes), as well as productivity and quality of
life. There are also associations between insomnia and being
overweight.

When Fred first started working as a pharmacist years ago, the
barbiturate and benzodiazepine medications were the most common
ones he handed out for the treatment of insomnia. These drugs, which
are also used to treat anxiety, include

- alprazolam (Xanax)

- clonazepam (Klonepin)

- temazepam (Restoril)

- triazolam (Halcion)

- oxazepam (Serax)

- lorazepam (Ativan)

- chlordiazepoxide (Librium)

- chlorazepate (Tranxene)

- prazepam (Centrax)

- quazepam (Dorax)

- estazalam (Prosom)

- diazepam (Valium)

- flurazepam (Dalmane)

The only difference between these drugs is how long it takes them to work and how long they stay around in your body. On average, they add an hour to your sleep time, and make you fall asleep about four minutes earlier.

Fred is always careful to counsel patients about the possible side effects from the benzodiazepines the day after taking them:

- drowsiness

- dizziness

- light-headedness

- problems with memory

He is especially worried about longer acting drugs, like Xanax, especially in older folks, since they can mess up your motor function. He tells his older patients that benzodiazepines increase their risk of falling and getting a hip fracture by 50%, and are associated with a 60% increase in road traffic accidents.

One of the newer sleeping pills, zopiclone (Imovane), has also been associated with an increased risk of road traffic accidents, and Fred tells people to be careful driving the day after taking a sleeping pill, no matter which one it is.

Fred still remembers when the newer generation of insomnia medications—zaleplon (Sonata), zolpidem (Ambien), eszopiclone (Lunesta), and zopiclone (Imovane), or "Z" drugs—act on specific subsets of the GABA receptor.

General side effects for all of these meds include:

- drowsiness

- memory impairment,

- headache

- dizziness

- nausea, and

- nervousness

Everyone always asks Fred which of the newer generation of sleeping pills, or "Z" drugs, is the best? Ever since he read *Before You Take that Pill: Why the Drug Industry May Be Bad For Your Health* (see Bibliography) he has been a little leary of the information pharmaceutical companies provide about their drugs. He likes to read the reviews coming out of the United Kingdom (UK) by the UK National Institute for Clinical Evidence (NICE), an unbiased governmental body that provides information on clinical treatments based on reviews by their experts of the evidence.

In a 2004 NICE review they reported that they found no difference between the different Z drugs (Sonata (zaleplon), Lunesta (eszopiclone), Ambien (zolpidem), or Imovane (zopiclone)) in efficacy, next-day impairment, or risk of withdrawal or dependence. As well, there were no benefits in terms of effectiveness or side effects compared to benzodiazepines. So Fred says it doesn't matter which one you take.

One of the freaky things Fred has heard about the Z drugs is stories about people who took them and starting walking in their sleep. They also did things like cook eggs or have sex and had absolutely no memory of it later.

Some of Fred's patients have also complained about their husbands who looked like they were asleep when they had sex and asked if there was a pill for that...but we are getting off course here.

Some people have also been known to drive in their sleep on Ambien. Remember that Kennedy guy?

One guy took an Ambien, had a glass of wine on a plane, and became a "monster." They had to divert the plane.

So Fred says don't drink on these drugs, ever.

Insomnia Medications: Risks and Benefits

Drug	Use	Common, benign side effects	Serious side effects	Life threatening side effects	Reasons not to take
Barbiturates *High Risk*					
phenobarbital (Luminal) *or* butabarbital (Butisol) *or* pentobarbital (Nembutal)	Insomnia	Drowsiness, lethargy, headache, dizziness	Problems breathing, delirium, depression	Allergic reaction, decreased blood counts (rare), respiratory depression, addiction	Allergy, addiction, depression
Antihistamines *Low Risk*					

Drug	Use	Common, benign side effects	Serious side effects	Life threatening side effects	Reasons not to take
hydroxyzine (Atarax, Vistaril)	Insomnia	Dry mouth, urinary retention	Confusion, night-mares, irritability	None	None
Benzodiazepines *Moderate Risk*					
alprazolam (Xanax) *or* clonazepam (Klonopin) *or* temazepam (Restoril) *or* oxazepam (Serax) *or* lorazepam (Ativan) *or* chlordiazepoxide (Librium) *or* clorazepate (Tranxene) *or* halazepam (Paxipam) *or* prazepam (Centrax) *or* quazepam (Doral) *or* estazolam (Prosom) *or* diazepam (Valium) *or* flurazepam (Dalmane)	Insomnia	Drowsiness	Dependency, memory loss, confusion	Hip fracture, driving accidents	History of addictions, memory impairment
triazolam (Halcion)	Insomnia	Drowsiness, early wake up	Dependency, memory loss, confusion	Hip fracture, driving accidents	History of addictions, memory impairment
Serotonin 1A Agonists					

Drug	Use	Common, benign side effects	Serious side effects	Life threatening side effects	Reasons not to take
Low Risk					
buspirone (Buspar)	Insomnia	Nausea, headache, light headedness	None	None	None
Z Drugs *Moderate Risk*					
zaleplon (Sonata) *or* zolpidem (Ambien) *or* zopiclone (Imovane)	Insomnia	Drowsiness, headache, nervousness	Memory loss	Sleep walking, driving accidents	Allergy to medication
eszopiclone (Lunesta)	Insomnia	Drowsiness, headache, nervousness, bad taste	Memory loss	Sleep walking, driving accidents	Allergy to medication
Melatonin Re-ceptor Agonists *Low Risk*					
ramelteon (Rozerem)	Insomnia	Headache, drowsiness, fatigue, dizziness, nausea	diarrhea	depression	Pregnancy or nursing

FIGURE 14: INSOMNIA MEDICATIONS: USES & RISKS

Adapted from BEFORE YOU TAKE THAT PILL, by J. Douglas Bremner, © 2008 J. Douglas Bremner, used by permission of Avery Publishing, an imprint of the Penguin Group.

In addition to these drugs, there are a handful of additional drugs that have sedative properties, and are prescribed and used "off label" for insomnia. These include drugs from allergy meds like antihistamines to antidepressants, some of which need a prescription and some can be bought in the pharmacy or "over the counter."

Fred's patients say they got the prescriptions from their doctors when they asked for something safer and with less potential for addiction or dependence than the Z drugs. He tells these people these drugs have active ingredients that work on other brain and body functions, so even the most benign of them (such as antihistamines) should be used with care.

The most commonly prescribed antihistamine for insomnia is hydroxyzine (Atarax, Vistaril). Over-the-counter diphenhydramine (Benadryl, Simply Sleep, Tylenol PM, Excedrin PM and their "store brand" counterparts) are often recommended by doctors as sleep aids, and are effective for many people. These medications are relatively free of potential for addiction or abuse.

Side effects are less common than for the benzodiazepines or Z drugs and include:

- dry mouth and urinary retention

- irritability, and

- more rarely, confusion, nightmares, and nervousness

Fred recommends them to people who don't have any money to go to a doctor. He also tells them that if you wake up in the middle of the night, that's normal, and don't worry about it.

The most effective therapy for the treatment of insomnia has been shown in studies to be cognitive behavioral therapy, much better than medication for sleeplessness and doesn't have any side effects. We'll deal with cognitive behavioral therapy in the next chapter.

Stimulants

Fred has noticed that a lot more adults are telling him that they've been diagnosed with an attention problem than the old days. In the old days, Fred only filled prescriptions like Ritalin or other stimulants for kids who had trouble paying attention in school and were diagnosed by their doctors as having Attention Deficit Disorder (ADD) or Attention Deficit and Hyperactivity Disorder (ADHD). Since there weren't that many kids being diagnosed back then, he kept Ritalin and his other medications for ADHD in the back of the pharmacy. But now that there's been a whopping increase in the use of these drugs, he's had to move them to the front.

And those drugs aren't just for the kiddies anymore. Whether it's something in the drinking water, a change in the way doctors diagnose things, or the increasing hecticness of modern life, Fred is seeing more and more adults being diagnosed with ADHD.

Fred's always noticed that a lot of the kids he saw with ADHD came from broken homes, were in foster care, or were victims of abuse. These days, a lot of the traumatized kids he knew are growing up but not growing out of their ADHD. He wants you to be safe if you get a prescription for one of these drugs, and the best way to do that is to know what they are, how they work, and possible side effects. The most common ADHD drugs are Ritalin, Adderall, and Strattera. So let's go.

Ritalin (methylphenidate, Methylin) is a stimulant medication that works by increasing the release of dopamine in the brain. That helps you concentrate better. Ritalin can suppress growth slightly in children. Other side effects include: palpitations, nervousness, rapid heart rate, loss of appetite, increased blood pressure, headache, upset stomach, and mood changes. High doses can cause psychosis. Extended release forms of methylphenidate or drugs that are essentially identical include Concerta, Metadate, and dexmethylphenidate (Focalin). These drugs are essentially identical to Ritalin, and have no demonstrated difference in efficacy.

Another stimulant medication used in the treatment of ADHD is the amphetamine Adderall (mixed amphetamine salts). Adderall is a mixture of two forms of amphetamine, and is marketed as a medication that only has to be taken once a day. Dextroamphetamine (Dexedrine) is comprised of one of the forms of amphetamine but is essentially the same thing as Adderall. These drugs also work by increasing dopamine in the brain. Adderall can suppress your appetite, which Fred says may or may not be a good thing. Like

Ritalin, Adderall probably has some long-term growth suppression effects in kids. Other side effects are palpitations, nervousness, rapid heart rate, and upset stomach. Fred's heard of cases of kids dying from cardiac arrest, but he's never seen that.

Another drug on Fred's ADHD shelf is atomoxetine (Strattera). Strattera blocks uptake of norepinephrine into the neuron. Strattera has the advantage over Adderall and Ritalin that it is not a stimulant and is therefore not associated with cardiac side effects. Side effects include indigestion, fatigue, dizziness, decreased appetite, and mood swings. Like Adderall, Strattera can inhibit growth in children.

It's time to say goodbye to Fred, and move on to psychological treatments for trauma. Fred doesn't know much about that, but he's seen some of his patients have good results, and if psychological treatments work better for some people than drugs (or helps augment the effects of drugs) he's all for it. After all, he's not a pill pusher.

Thanks, Fred. Bye!

Chapter 10: Psychological Therapy for Psychological Trauma

This chapter covers psychological treatments for trauma, which trauma survivors often find very useful.

Most psychological therapies involve some degree of mental exposure to the traumatic event in a safe, controlled environment, with an evaluation of their personal response to the exposure. This means the patient will be asked to recount his traumatic event, and talk about his thoughts, feelings, and understandings (or misunderstandings) about the event.

Examples of thoughts would be "I couldn't believe this was happening to me" or "my mother was just outside but I couldn't call out to her." Feelings would include anger, fear, disgust, and helplessness. Perceptions would include "I deserved this because I shouldn't have been there at that time."

Before starting therapy, important factors such as suicidality, substance abuse, panic, and disorganized thinking, must be evaluated and dealt with.

The next phase is educating both the patient, and the family and friends of the person affected, as discussed in more detail above.

Cognitive Behavioral Therapy (CBT)

Cognitive Behavioral Therapy (CBT) involves a focus on the thoughts, feelings, and cognitions related to the traumatic event. It doesn't spend as much time talking about things not related to the trauma, for example, your feelings about your family, or things of that sort. CBT tries to correct negative or distorted thoughts or cognitions about the actual trauma.

Many CBT therapists will evaluate your level of distress using something like the Subjective Units of Distress Scale (SUDS). The

SUDS asks how distressed you are feeling right now on a scale of 0 (not distressed at all) to 100 (extremely distressed). Therapists will typically administer the SUDS at the beginning and end of a therapy session, and after going through evoking imagery of a traumatic event.

Specifics of the CBT technique involve taking one element of the trauma at a time (known as "desensitization") so that the traumatic event is not too overwhelming.

Most therapists will also teach you relaxation techniques (deep breathing, muscle stretching, and relaxation) that can help you get through the imagery of a traumatic memory.

Another technique involves developing a mental image in your mind of a safe and happy place...maybe a place on the beach, or up on a mountain top. First you develop the image of that place so that you can quickly return to it. Then if you get too overwhelmed with your traumatic image, you can switch to the safe place to bring down your anxiety level.

We talk more about these techniques in Chapter 11, "Tools for Coping with Stress."

In CBT, exposure to the imagery of the traumatic event occurs repeatedly over the course of the sessions, with administration of the SUDS, to show a decrease in distress related to the traumatic images. Sometimes therapists will ask you to do "homework" where you invoke the images at home and do your own self ratings. Exposure therapy is usually pretty effective if people can stick with it.

Cognitive Behavioral Therapy for the Treatment of Insomnia

As we pointed out in the last chapter, cognitive behavioral therapy is also useful in the treatment of insomnia. To truly benefit from cognitive therapy, it is preferable if you can have a few sessions with therapist trained in this specialized therapy.

The first step is to replace negative thoughts ("I can't sleep without medications") with more positive ones ("If I take the time to relax, I can get to sleep without help from pills.") The underlying theory is that you "retrain" your brain to learn to sleep peacefully and deeply again.

Changing sleep habits is the second piece of cognitive therapy. For example,

- using the bed and bedroom only for sleep (no working or TV-watching in bed; insomniacs often spend too much time in bed trying to sleep, and the best thing to do is to get out of bed and read for a while or listen to soft music),

- setting and maintaining a regular sleep schedule,

- eliminating daytime naps,

- minimizing or avoiding altogether caffeine, alcohol, stimulants, and heavy or extremely spicy meals four to six hours before going to bed, and

- relaxation techniques such as progressive muscle relaxation often help. It involves alternately contracting individual muscles and relaxing with exhalation; the individual goes progressively through the body one muscle group at a time.

Behavioral changes are highly effective, and, best of all, persist for a longer period of time than drug therapy. About 80% of patients will show improvement. The time to fall asleep is reduced from sixty-five minutes to thirty-five minutes, an increase in sleep time of thirty minutes, and improved subjective ratings of sleep quality.

Since long-term use of sleeping pills is not recommended, people with chronic insomnia really need to make the effort to get sleep behavioral therapy treatment, or, at a minimum, educate themselves through reading or online about the principles promoted in CBT programs for insomnia.

Meditation and gentle yoga can also help some people fall asleep more easily as part of a cognitive therapy program or on their own.

Systematic Desensitization and Imaginal Exposure Therapies

Two techniques closely related to CBT and often used together include systematic desensitization and imaginal exposure therapies.

In systematic desensitization, there is pairing of a reminder of the trauma with relaxation, so that the anxiety associated with thinking about the traumatic event is inhibited by relaxation. When you become anxious, you are instructed to erase the scene, relax, and then imagine the scenario again. This is repeated until anxiety is no longer associated with the imagination.

In imaginal exposure therapy, to enhance the vividness of the memory, you are asked to imagine the event in your mind and focus on your thoughts and emotions as if the event were happening now. Instructions for imaginal therapy might go something like this:

- I want you to close your eyes and begin to talk about the assault.

- Talk about it in the first person, as if it is happening to you right now.

- As you're talking, picture the story in your mind, and describe what is happening.

- Describe it in as much detail as possible, including what you're doing, what he's doing, what you're thinking and feeling.

- Try not to let go of the image, even if it's upsetting to you, and

- We will talk about it after the exposure is finished.

Other treatments effective for PTSD fall into the category of anxiety management, which we discuss next.

Stress Inoculation Training (SIT)

Stress Inoculation Training (SIT) involves several anxiety-management techniques, including:

- psychoeducation

- muscle relaxation training

- breathing retraining

- role playing

- covert modeling

- guided self-dialogue

- thought stopping

This treatment program has been shown to be effective in the treatment of PTSD.

Eye Movement Desensitization and Reprocessing (EMDR) Therapy

Another type of therapy that has been shown to work is Eye Movement Desensitization and Reprocessing (EMDR) therapy.

This involves having patients follow a moving finger while visualizing their trauma. Newer versions of EMDR have involved other methods like tapping on alternative shoulders during re-exposure to the trauma. Controlled studies have shown the usefulness of this technique for treating trauma.

Hypnosis in the Treatment of Psychological Trauma

Although hypnosis has had a controversial place in the treatment of stress-related psychiatric disorders, in the hands of competent and trained professionals, it does serve a potentially useful role.

Memories not available to consciousness due to processes such as dissociative amnesia may be accessed through hypnosis. Some studies have shown that hypnosis may lead to an improvement in PTSD symptoms.

When memories that were not previously fully available are brought into consciousness, they can be processed for the emotional and cognitive content, and gradually integrated into the patient's normal storehouse of memories.

This process must be performed with caution because the reintroduction of traumatic memories into consciousness may be associated with a feeling of upset and an increase in psychiatric symptoms. Some therapists get written informed consent from patients who are to undergo hypnosis, so that these patients can recognize the potential limitations and pitfalls.

Psychodynamic Therapy

Although psychodynamic therapy has not been subjected to as much research, we are firm believers in psychologically-oriented or psychodynamic therapy. This typically involves meeting one-on-one with a therapist for once a week and talking about things related to the trauma, as well as things in the here and now and how they are connected to the original trauma. It also involves evaluating the thoughts and feelings you develop about the therapist and the therapy itself.

Psychodynamic therapy helps trauma patients understand what the meaning of their trauma is for them as human beings. It also involves a lot of the techniques involved in the therapies listed above, like examining the basis in reality for a lot of the cognitions related to the trauma, or anxiety related to memories of the trauma.

You will likely be in therapy for longer — months or even years — than CBT, which usually only lasts a matter of weeks.

Group Therapy

Our guess is that you won't find many people in therapy groups who will tell you to just get over it or to just snap out of it.

Groups are best when they are led by two mental health professionals with training and experience in running group therapy.

Adding Therapy to START-NOW

Different therapists have different orientations, but successful therapists all share in common a commitment to, and belief in, their methods, and a professional and empathic approach to their clients. Studies have shown that the ability of the therapist and the individual fit with the client are more important than which of many theoretical orientations are used. A big part of therapy is connecting with the therapist, honestly sharing your experiences and learning that you are not an alien or alone in the world.

Therapy can help you at all stages of the START-NOW process, from learning a feeling of safety, getting validation for yourself as a person and the magnitude of your psychological trauma, getting grounded when you are still interacting with crazy-making family members, and joining you in your journey to revise your personal history.

By talking about how you relate to your therapist, you can learn about how you relate to other people in your life, and how your trauma has affected those interactions. Your therapist may be the first person you talk to about your trauma, and if he or she is professional, you can count on them to not tell you to "just get over it," "snap out of it," or "move on." After all, listening to you in the context of their knowledge and training is why they get paid.

How Therapy Works on the Brain

Psychological therapies are probably effective because of the way they act on the brain to reverse the effects of trauma. As discussed above, one of the hallmarks of psychological trauma is an inability to extinguish or wipe out fear responses with reminders of the trauma. In full-blown PTSD patients, this can become very disabling, to the point where it interferes with all their daily activities. For these patients, dysfunction in the prefrontal cortex leads to an inability to extinguish traumatic memories through inhibition of activity in the amygdala. One of the roles of these therapies is to help the brain to inhibit or extinguish traumatic memories through techniques such as gradual exposure to traumatic reminders in the supportive context of therapy. We talked about what these brain regions are and what they do in an earlier chapter, so you might want to go back and review that part now.

We discussed above the laboratory model of conditioned fear responses, how pairing an unconditioned stimulus (e.g., an electric shock) with a conditioned stimulus (e.g., bright light) leads to a fear reaction to the conditioned stimulus ("bright light") alone. With repeated exposure to the conditioned stimulus, there is a decrease in fear responding, related to an inhibition of the amygdala (which plays a critical role in learning fear) by the prefrontal cortex.

In a similar way in normal individuals, fear responses to reminders of the trauma normally become extinguished with repeated exposure to reminders of the trauma. However, for PTSD patients, dysfunction in the prefrontal cortex leads to an inability to extinguish traumatic memories through inhibition of activity in the amygdala.

One of the roles of behavioral therapies is to facilitate the ability of the brain to inhibit or extinguish traumatic memories, through techniques such as gradual exposure to traumatic reminders, in the supportive context of a therapeutic environment.

If You Cannot Afford Therapy

Since PTSD or depression related to trauma can affect our ability to work or to reach our full potential of productivity, we often encounter trauma patients who are unable to afford therapy.

If you don't have insurance and/or a high-paying job (or any kind of job), you might not be able to afford visits to a medical doctor or psychiatrist (who is also a medical doctor) or prescription medications.

You can explore some options:

- If you can afford even a fifteen-minute visit you might be able to get a psychiatrist to give you a free sample of one of the newer antidepressants left for them by the pharmaceutical sales people who frequently stop by their offices.

- If you can afford even a fifteen-minute visit you might be able to get a psychiatrist to give you a free sample of one of the newer antidepressants left for them by the pharmaceutical sales people who frequently stop by their offices.

- Also, some of the drug companies have compassionate care programs you can sign up for to get free medications.

- Finally, you can get a generic version of an antidepressant and buy it at Walmart for about $44.00 a month. There are other discount deals available at other stores you might want to keep an eye out for.

- If you have trouble sleeping you can get some of the over-the-counter medications we talked about in the prior chapter like diphenhydramine (Benadryl).

- You can also do things like exercise, which is free and helps mental symptoms.

For psychotherapy, you should be aware that different people charge different rates. For instance, many social workers charge less than psychologists or psychiatrists. You can also look into getting free treatment. If you are a veteran with PTSD, you might be eligible for treatment at a Veterans Affairs (VA) hospital. You can call Scheduling and ask for a mental health evaluation, and they can refer you to their mental health clinic, or sometimes refer you to outside treatment that they pay for.

Most states and counties also have free mental health care paid for by the government. For instance, in Georgia we have Community Service Boards (CSBs) in every county that are supported by the government. These types of treatment vary from state to state and may require copayment depending on what they decide is your ability to pay based on something called a means test.

If you have an alcohol or drug problem you can attend Alcoholic Anonymous (AA) meetings for free. These are located everywhere and involve groups of alcoholics who meet and give each other support. They also involve assigning you a sponsor, who is a peer who will monitor your recovery. There are similar programs for drug problems. For family members of people with substance abuse problems there are Al-anon meetings. Many trauma patients go to Alanon meetings even if they didn't have a family member with a drug problem, because they find that a lot of the same issues are relevant to their own background of dealing with psychological trauma or growing up in an emotionally damaging family.

Finally, other than the cost of this book (which you either already purchased or are borrowing from a friend) you can do the START-NOW program for free. You can also download the workbook for free from http://www.dougbremner.com/startnowworkbook.pdf.

Do it now!

The Bottom Line for the Treatment of Trauma

The bottom line is that if you suffer from PTSD or depression related to psychological trauma, and you can afford it, you should give psychotherapy a try. There are a number of different types of therapy that have been shown to work, but the most important thing is to find a therapist you feel comfortable with who is professional and confident in their ability to help you.

Many therapists will post a bio on their websites describing their training and approach to patients which can be very useful assisting you with finding an appropriate therapist. If you are seeking therapy related to certain circumstances, for example child abuse, or post-war trauma, check with local groups who support people struggling with these problems, or consult the resources in Appendix B to this book, and see which therapists they have found to be successful for their members. Make appointments with a few different therapists before you decide to go with a particular one.

In our opinion, for therapy to be useful, at some point there needs to be a re-examination of the trauma, how you felt at the time, and what you thought and experienced. If you are not comfortable with a therapist, or you feel s/he is acting in an unprofessional manner, feel free to try someone else. After all, it's your money.

As well as psychotherapy, antidepressant medications may be useful in the treatment of PTSD and depression related to psychological trauma. In general, the SSRIs have fewer side effects that were typical of the older generation of tricyclics. They can also be associated with a significant inhibition of libido, which can be a real problem if you are in a relationship. Atypical antidepressants like Wellbutrin can overcome those sexual side effects. (See Chapter 9 for a list of drugs and their side effects.) If you do take SSRIs, start out at half the dose that the manufacturer recommends as a starting dose, and increase and decrease the dose at very small increments, to avoid the mood swings and suicidal thoughts that seem to be associated with too rapid changes in medication.

In general, all antidepressants are equally effective, so the choice of antidepressants becomes based on side effects and costs. The dual reuptake inhibitors venlafaxine and duloxetine do seem to have a slight advantage in terms of efficacy over SSRIs and the other antidepressants like tricyclics, but the suicide risk may counter the added efficacy.

The bottom line of the research on treatments for the mental health effects of psychological trauma and the effects of psychological trauma on the brain is that there is hope. Symptoms related to trauma are mediated by the brain. If we can reverse these brain changes, we can reverse the symptoms. If you take an active role in your recovery, you will do better. One way you can do this by engaging in psychotherapy, possibly adding medication, improving your diet and lifestyle, and by learning tools for coping with stress, which we discuss in the next chapter.

CHAPTER 11: TOOLS FOR COPING WITH STRESS

This chapter covers tools for coping with stress. They don't take a lot of time, you don't have to be a genius to do them, you don't (necessarily) have to take drugs or see a doctor, and best of all, they are free (except for the cost of this book, which you've presumably already paid for.)

No matter how bad or overwhelming your stress is, or how terrible your mental suffering or the things you have been through, in our experience, everyone will be able to make at least a little progress in getting on top of their stress if they follow the teachings of this book. And some will benefit even more. This chapter outlines specific tools for coping with stress, and is a complement to the START-NOW program outlined later.

So let's pack up and get going.

Identify the Sources of Your Stress

The first thing to do is to identify where your stress is coming from:

- Is it what we call daily, situational stress?

- Are you stressed by recurrent memories of a traumatic event of the past?

- Or are you suffering from a more complex mental disorder, like depression, PTSD, or another anxiety disorder?

Figuring out which it is can help you to reduce stress by eliminating the triggers that cause stress.

If you have PTSD, being around reminders of the original traumatic event can increase stress and anxiety. In panic disorder,

FIGURE 15: FINDING THE SOURCES OF STRESS

which can also stem from a traumatic event, a fear of having a panic attack in public can cause chronic stress or make you afraid to leave your home or be in public places.

Knowing the specific causes of the stress, and recognizing that the fear or worry may be coming from the disorder rather than a real threat, will be helpful. You can read about the symptoms of these disorders in earlier chapters of this book, or seek the help of a mental health professional for diagnosis. In any case, all of these anxiety disorders will benefit from knowledge of the tools for coping with stress outlined in this chapter.

Psychotherapy for Stress

How do you treat stress reactions?

As touched on in Chapter Ten, one of the ways to treat stress reactions caused by specific events is exposure therapy. This is a type of treatment done with a mental health professional where you are gradually exposed to something that causes you stress and anxiety until you get to the point where it doesn't cause as much stress.

With repeated sessions of going over the same event, the stress and anxiety is reduced, and this generalizes into your daily life. You can also identify the cues that trigger stress and anxiety, and learn to avoid them.

Deep Breathing

One tool for coping with stress which you can do on your own or with the help of a therapist is deep breathing. People in the mental health field are becoming more and more aware of how important focusing on your breathing is as a useful tool for reducing stress.

Try this exercise (if you are on a train you can cut out some of the parts that make you feel like you look ridiculous):

1. Sit comfortably with your back straight. If you feel more comfortable that way, lie on the floor.

2. Put one hand on your chest and the other on your stomach.

3. Focus on your breath going in and out of your body.

4. Breathe deeply from your stomach, rather than taking shallow breaths in your chest, getting as much fresh air as possible in your lungs. This will get more oxygen into your lungs, which will make you feel less tense, short of breath, and anxious.

5. Now breathe in through your nose.

The hand on your stomach should rise, while the hand on your chest doesn't move much. If you are lying on the floor, you can put something on your stomach and watch it rise and fall.

6. Breathe out through your mouth, pushing out as much air as you can while squeezing your stomach muscles. The hand on your stomach should move in as you breathe out, but your other hand shouldn't move much.

7. Continue to breathe in through your nose and out through your mouth.

8. Try to inhale enough so that your stomach rises and falls.

9. Count slowly as you exhale.

Progressive Muscle Relaxation

Progressive muscle relaxation involves progressively moving through your body and tensing and relaxing all of your muscles. It will help you learn where you carry your stress in the different muscle groups of your body, and to spot when stress is causing your muscles to become tense. For this one, you can lie on the floor and take off your shoes, or if you are in a public place, you can do it while sitting:

1. Start at your feet and move your way up your body.

2. Take a deep breath and hold it.

3. Push your toes down like you are stepping on the gas as hard as you can for five seconds.

4. Now slowly relax your muscles as you let your breath leave your body.

5. Breathe out.

6. Sit there for a few seconds breathing in and out while focusing on your body and how it feels.

7. Now, pull your toes up toward your nose as hard as you can.

8. Breathe out.

9. Continue to breathe in with muscle tightening and out with relaxing with short resting periods after relaxing.

10. Tighten the muscles in your calves. Breathe in. Relax your muscles. Breathe out.

11. Now tighten the muscles the ones in your thighs. Breathe in. Relax your muscles. Breathe out.

12. Tighten the muscles in your buttocks. Breathe in. Relax your muscles. Breathe out.

13. Tighten your stomach muscles. Breathe in. Relax your muscles. Breathe out.

14. Scrunch your shoulders up toward your head. Breathe in. Relax your muscles. Breathe out.

15. Squeeze your hands. Breathe in. Relax your muscles. Breathe out.

16. Pull your hands up to your shoulders. Breathe in. Relax your muscles. Breathe out.

17. Now stretch your arms out straight. Breathe in. Relax your muscles. Breathe out.

18. Pull your head down to your chest. Breathe in. Relax your muscles. Breathe out.

19. Push your head to the right, all the way until it is tight. Breathe in. Relax your muscles. Breathe out.

20. Push your head to the left. Breathe in. Relax your muscles. Breathe out.

21. Now go through the different muscle groups in your face, one-by-one.

When you are done, remain silent and focus on your breath going in and out for three minutes. Feel the tension leave your body every time you breathe out.

If you want, you can visualize a peaceful scene on the beach or in the mountains. See, smell, hear, and feel everything that is happening in your imagined scene. How do you feel? Better?

Do this every day for a week or two at the end of your work day, early in the morning, or whatever works for you. In time, you will be able to do a quick version of this in the middle of your busy day.

Guided Visual Imagery

Speaking of visualizing a peaceful scene on the beach, guided visual imagery is another great tool for coping with stress.

Guided visual imagery involves imagining a peaceful scene where you can let go of your stress. Think of a place you have been or make up something new in your mind. You might want to think about a tropical beach, a place in the mountains, or a place you liked to go to be alone and feel safe when you were in childhood. Close your eyes and bring the scene into your mind.

For instance, say you see yourself in an alpine meadow. The sky is blue with a few wispy white clouds in the sky. The grey granite of rocky peaks rises all around. There is a slight breeze and the lazy buzzing of some insects far away. The short green alpine grass and yellow and white alpine flowers rustle in the breeze. You are all alone. Feel the wind slightly rustling your hair and the sun upon your cheek. Picture the mountain scene or wherever you have decided to go as vividly as possible. See the colors, smell the smells, here the sounds, and feel the sensations of the scene you are in. Try and bring in as many sensory processes as possible. As you visualize the scene, focus on your breathing, and feel your stress and worries slip away.

Mindful Meditation

Mindful meditation is rapidly growing in popularity as a tool for coping with stress.

In our research studies, we have found mindful meditation to be an effective treatment for PTSD, both in Iraq vets as well as PTSD related to other traumas. It also reverses some of the changes in the brain associated with trauma. Mindful meditation incorporates some of the tools mentioned above, including focusing on the breath and the body. Mindfulness involves being fully present in the current time and letting thoughts about the future and the past slip away.

The process involves a detached awareness of one's own thoughts and breathing without being overly critical of one's own thoughts or over-thinking an experience. If a judgmental thought about your own anxiety or stress reactions or behavior comes into your mind, you don't fight it, you just note it and then let it move away.

Mindfulness is useful because it removes the process of dwelling on the past, on thinking about things we could have done, or worrying about what will happen in the future. That is because there is nothing we can do to change the past, and in the vast majority of cases, little we can do to change the future. We waste an inordinate amount of time thinking about these things, which raises our stress levels. Mindfulness is a way of teaching yourself to focus on what is happening right now, whether in your mind or your body, which is associated with a release of tension and a calming of the spirit.

By monitoring your thoughts, you bring yourself into the present.

In the body scan, you focus your attention on various parts of your body. Like progressive muscle relaxation, you start with your feet and work your way up. However, instead of tensing and relaxing your muscles, you simply focus on the way each part of your body feels without labeling the sensations as either "good" or "bad."

You don't have to be seated or still to meditate. In walking meditation, mindfulness involves being focused on the physicality of each step — the sensation of your feet touching the ground, the rhythm of your breath while moving, and feeling the wind against your face.

Try practicing mindful eating. If you reach for food when you're under stress or gulp your meals down in a rush, try eating mindfully. Sit down at the table and focus your full attention on the meal (no TV, newspapers, or eating on the run). Eat slowly, taking the time to fully enjoy and concentrate on each bite. We can learn something from the Slow Food movement in Italy.

Mindfulness meditation is not equal to zoning out. It takes effort to maintain your concentration and to bring it back to the present moment when your mind wanders or you start to drift off, but with regular practice, mindfulness meditation actually changes the brain, strengthening the areas associated with joy and relaxation, and weakening those involved in negativity and stress.

You can train yourself through books like this and self work or sign up for classes that usually meet weekly as a group for eight sessions with homework in between.

Using Tools for Coping with Stress

The tools for coping with stress are not meant to be used alone. We see them as complementary tools for the START-NOW program, better lifestyles, and possibly psychotherapy or medication. For instance, if you become overwhelmed by anxiety when re-visiting your trauma, you may need to use deep breathing or guided visual imagery to help you get re-grounded. Every step of the START-NOW program may require use of some of the tools.

Give them a try!

CHAPTER 12: BETTER LIFESTYLES AS A TOOL FOR RECOVERY FROM PSYCHOLOGICAL TRAUMA

Making changes in your diet and lifestyle is an important part of your recovery from psychological trauma. Not only will this improve your physical health, but it will benefit your mental health as well.

Eating right, exercising, and changing other aspects of your lifestyle can affect how you feel, and how you feel about yourself. Making these changes have also been shown to be useful in the treatment of mental disorders, like depression and PTSD.

Psychological Trauma: Strikes Against You in Terms of Health

People with a history of psychological trauma have a number of strikes against them when it comes to health. Trauma leads to an increase in risky behaviors that threaten good health. For instance, women with a history of childhood sexual abuse have been shown to have an increase in obesity.

Childhood trauma is also associated with an increase in smoking, using drugs, using too many prescription medications like sedatives and pain killers, and drinking too much alcohol.

Dr. Rob Anda, a doctor and scientist we collaborate with at the Centers for Disease Control (CDC) (it's right next door to Emory University, where we work and have our Clinical Neuroscience Research Unit (ECNRU), in Atlanta, Georgia), did a study that showed that childhood trauma increased the risk for intravenous drug abuse by *ten-fold!* That's a greater risk than getting lung cancer from smoking.

Benefits of Exercise for Trauma Victims

Exercise helps trauma victims in more ways than one. Not only will it improve your health, but it will also make you feel better. That is because when you are on your path toward recovery from psychological trauma, you will generate a lot of "fight or flight" responses in yourself, as you follow the START-NOW program and do things like re-visit and re-write your trauma. The best way to deal with this is to burn off this extra energy through vigorous exercise.

How much should you exercise?

We recommend that you exercise at least three times a week for thirty minutes. You might say, but I don't like running. Even a brisk walk counts as exercise.

Studies have shown that exercise is an excellent treatment for mental disorders like depression and PTSD. In fact, exercise is as good as Zoloft (sertraline) for depression! Other studies showed that exercise works as well as antidepressants for the treatment of PTSD. Even just a few hours of walking per week helps. Exercise results in increased vitality and life satisfaction, and decreased levels of stress. Exercise results in a surge of serotonin, the neurotransmitter which make us feel good right, after working out, as well as a long-term mood shift once you've started exercising regularly.

Exercise also has positive effects on the brain, reversing the effects of trauma. Exercise results in increased growth in brain cells in the hippocampus, the opposite of the effects of stress. This is a good non-chemical way of helping restore your brain to the condition it was prior to your trauma. Regular exercise has favorable effects on the immune system as well, which may promote health, especially if you are stressed and/or depressed.

Exercise is far less expensive, and more easily accessible, than medication and psychotherapy. Plus, it has none of the side effects, such as sexual dysfunction, as seen with some antidepressants. Indeed, the "side effects" of using exercise as your antidepressant are beneficial to your general well-being:

- improved heart health,

- increased strength,

- lessening depression and anxiety, and

- weight loss.

Healthy Eating

Healthy eating is another crucial part of your better lifestyles program. We think you should cook your own food, because that is the best way to have fresh and healthy ingredients and avoid preservatives. Making your own meals is also essential to making sure that you eat a lot of fruits and vegetables, which are key to good health.

People who are depressed and/or have a history of childhood psychological trauma have an increase in risk for obesity as adults. Eating diets high in fat can interfere with the formation of serotonin, a neurotransmitter implicated in depression, which might affect your mood.

Studies have also shown that ingestion of fat results in a temporary drop in mood. Remember the guy from the movie *Super Size Me*, Morgan Spurlock? He was practically psycho after a month of eating nothing but McDonald's food.

It is important to teach yourself to cook, so that you can stay away from fast food restaurants, where you are almost sure to get too much fat and too many calories, and not enough of the things you need like fresh fruits and vegetables. Relying on fast food restaurants and eating a poor diet will increase your weight and have a negative effect on your mood. That in turn will be a barrier in your pathway toward recovery from psychological trauma.

A long time ago people noticed that people from Italy live longer and seemed to get less disease than people in the U.S. This led to the idea that maybe something about differences in diet, which came to be known as the Mediterranean Diet, could account for this.

The Mediterranean Diet is associated with sustained weight loss. This diet is:

- high in vegetables, legumes, fruits, nuts, cereals, and fish,

- low in meat and poultry and dairy products,

- recommended alcohol consumption of ten to 50 grams (1-4 glasses of wine) per day for men, and five to twenty-five grams (1-2 glasses of wine) for women

- The diet substitutes unsaturated fats (olive oil) for saturated and monounsaturated fats (butter, animal fat).

The Mediterranean Diet:

- reduces heart disease, stroke, diabetes, and cancer risk,

- prolongs life (following the Mediterranean Diet is associated with a reduction in mortality by one half over a four-year time period in some populations),

- cuts the number of heart attacks in half in patients with heart disease, an effect that in one study was twice as good as medication treatment.

- Overall, the effects of these diets were superior to medications for weight loss and the prevention of heart disease and diabetes, with fewer side effects and more positive effects on well-being.

See the figure below, provided courtesy of Oldways Preservation and Exchange Trust, a nonprofit foundation dedicated to promotion of the Mediterranean Diet and other healthy behaviors. Diet modifications including following the Mediterranean Diet have been shown to have a protective effect against the development of several neurological disorders, including Parkinson's Disease (PD), Multiple Sclerosis, Mild Cognitive Impairment (MCI) and Alzheimer's Disease.

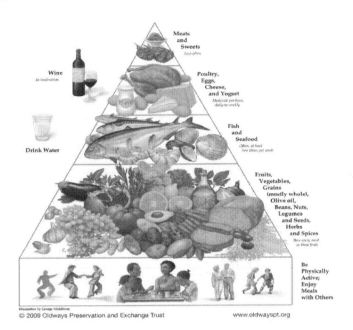

FIGURE 16: MEDITERRANEAN DIET FOOD PYRAMID

The diet is high in olive oil, fish, nuts, and breads, and low in red meat. Figure courtesy of Oldways Preservation and Exchange Trust. http://oldwayspt.org/resources/heritage-pyramids/mediterranean-diet-pyramid Copyright © 2012 Oldways Preservation and Exchange Trust, used with permission.

Adding folate to the diet (associated with a reduction in homocysteine in the blood) helps with symptoms of depression, and at least one study showed that taking omega-3 fatty acid supplements helped symptoms of bipolar disorder.

Get Your Substance Abuse Under Control

Many survivors of psychological trauma use alcohol to reduce their anxiety and stress symptoms.

Has alcohol become a problem for you? It isn't always easy to tell. Alcohol dependence is defined as the situation where you have to drink more to get the same effect. Same goes for drug use.

If you are trying to cut back without success, that may be a clue that consumption of alcohol is getting out of control. I often look for a history of arrest for Driving Under the Influence (DUI) as evidence that someone's drinking is out of control. Getting into an accident, being late for work, missing work, or getting into trouble at work because of drinking or using drugs are also indicators of a problem. Being often told by friends and family that your drinking or substance use is a problem should be taken as a warning sign. You won't be able to benefit from the steps of the START-NOW program if you are under the influence of drugs or alcohol, so you should address this first.

Symptoms of Alcohol and Substance Abuse and Dependence
• Arrest for Driving Under the Influence (DUI)
• Missing days at work or being late to work because of drug or alcohol abuse
• Needing increasingly larger amounts of the substance for the same effect
• Trying to cut down but not being able to
• Being told repeatedly by friends and family that your drug or alcohol abuse is a problem
• Getting into accidents or sustaining injuries as a result of drug or alcohol abuse
• Not being able to remember what happened or having blackouts during drinking or drug use

FIGURE 17: SYMPTOMS OF ALCOHOL ABUSE

The Risks of Prescription Drugs

Although some prescription medications are often helpful for trauma-related mental conditions, others can be a problem, or mixing them with alcohol or drugs can have dangerous effects. More people die in the U.S. every year now from overdoses of prescription medications (usually sleeping pills, sedatives, and pain meds) than from illegal drugs or car accidents. Big offenders are the pain medication oxycodone, and benzodiazepines like Valium (Diazepam) and Xanax (Alprazolam).

Who are these people that are dying from prescription drugs?

More than half of all Americans are now on at least one prescription drug, and 81% take some kind of pill. We spend twice as much money on drugs, and take twice as many drugs as other countries, but still our healthcare outcomes are second to last amongst industrialized countries. Even England is better, even though the English have a worse diet, and smoke and drink more than Americans.

As discussed in my book, *Before You Take That Pill: Why the Drug Industry May Be Bad For Your Health: Risks and Side Effects You Won't*

Find on the Label of Commonly Prescribed Drugs, Vitamins and Supplements, (published by Penguin Press in 2008), studies show that for many conditions, including heart disease and diabetes, making changes in diet and lifestyle are often better than taking prescription medications.

The Bottom Line on Better Lifestyles

We recommend that you cook most of your own meals, eat fish twice a week, drink water instead of soda, use a lot of olive oil, eat a lot of fresh fruit and vegetables, add nuts to your dishes, and exercise three times a week, even if it is just taking long walks.

These changes will not only improve your physical health, they will reduce stress-related symptoms, symptoms of depression and PTSD, and help you burn off extra fight or flight energy that are a by-product of following your path toward recovery from psychological trauma.

CHAPTER 13: WORKING TOGETHER AS COUPLES

Psychological trauma affects not only the individuals who are exposed to trauma, but also intimate partners closest to them. This chapter is about being in an intimate relationship with someone with a history of psychological trauma, and is written for both the trauma survivors and their partners. That's because you will journey on the path to recovery from psychological trauma together.

Intimate partners are a critical component of recovery from psychological trauma. That's why we think it is so important to make the bond between couples stronger—to help them on their joint path toward recovery from psychological trauma.

If you cut yourself, or break a bone, it takes time to heal, right? Why should it be any different for psychological trauma? Strengthening the partner bond is a key aspect of recovery from psychological trauma, because trauma victims need that intimate connection to begin to heal.

This chapter is about working together to achieve your shared goals of recovering from trauma, strengthening your relationship, and achieving greater intimacy. These goals are all inter-related.

Effects of Psychological Trauma on Relationships

Traumatic stress can take a big hit on relationships. Avoidance, retreat from other people, emotional numbing, and irritability can introduce problems into any relationship, and these are all behaviors that are closely linked to psychological trauma. If someone has PTSD and/or depression, the problem is even worse.

This is unfortunate, since the most important thing in recovery from psychological trauma is to have the love and support of our partner. When we are under siege, we need close and supportive relationships, and we need encouragement to recover from psychological trauma.

How Do You Make Great Relationships?

How do you strengthen relationships? Everyone assumes that they know how to "do" relationships with others. But is that really the case?

Not really. You can learn how to have great relationships, just like you can learn to play the piano or drive a car. We think that everybody should take a class on relationships at some point, preferably before you get married. For survivors of psychological trauma, it's even more important.

So what makes for a great relationship?

The most important things are honesty, trust, equality, respect, mutual support, shared goals, flexibility, and friendship. We will go over each of these, one at a time. While these things are important for everyone, they are especially important for psychological trauma survivors.

Sharing With Your Partner Promotes Greater Intimacy

You don't have to share everything about yourself with everyone, but you do need to share with your partner. Couples need to share thoughts and feelings openly. The more you can share about your thoughts and feelings with your partner, the greater intimacy you will have in your relationship. It also helps to counter-act the tendency that traumatized people have to feel like they are aliens, are different from other people, or that no one can understand or what they feel and have been through.

Building Trust

The foundation of every relationship is trust, and for psychological trauma survivors, in whom the ability to trust is wounded, this is even more important. If you feel like you can't trust your partner, the relationship rests on unstable ground. Trust is

FIGURE 18: BUILDING TRUST

something that grows with time.

How do you build trust?

It takes time and effort to build up the trust in your marriage and maintain it. Before you start doing things like figuring out the password of your partner's email account and reading her emails, consider what effect that will have on the trust in your marriage. You are sending a message that you don't trust her.

You have only so much "trust capital" to spend, so don't use it all at once.

Open communication is good, even the bad stuff. People would rather hear what is going on with you, even if sounds negative, because being honest with your partner deepens the intimacy, and we all crave greater intimacy with others.

We want to be connected!

That shared intimacy is key to the recovery from psychological trauma. When things go wrong and you cheat on your partner with someone else, that has a serious effect on trust. It may take time, but trust issues can be repaired.

Sharing Equal Roles in a Relationship

It is critical that the two persons in a partnership have equal roles.

One person may bring home the big paycheck, and the other one is a stay-at-home mom without an income, but the different roles should be seen as equal. Taking care of the children is not less important than working in a job for pay. Partners must work together as a team. You need to make all decisions together and have equal input, whether it is about money, children, or other issues.

Have Common Dreams

Have a shared dream with your partner. Couples that dream together grow together and stay together. Talk to your partner about your dreams and find some that you have in common and can get excited about together:

- When do you want to retire?

- Where?

- What kind of aspirations do you have for your kids?

- Do you want them to have the opportunity to go to college?

What's your bucket list?

These are all things that need to be discussed early on and openly. Working at cross purposes with your partner can be exhausting. So don't do it!

The Importance of Shared Goals

Related to having shared dreams is having shared goals. It is important for couples to explicitly outline their goals and come to an agreement about them. Make a list of what you would like to accomplish together:

- Where do you want to live?

- Does a big house matter to you?

- How many kids do you want?

- What would you like for them to accomplish?

All of these things are important to discuss with your partner.

It's also important to be ready to revise your family goals when you need to. To do that, you will need to have frank and open discussions with your partner on a regular basis.

Having shared experiences with your partner will build up trust and make your bond stronger. Try to find fun things to do with your partner. Have a store of positive memories for the bad times.

Your partner should be your best friend. Be open and willing to lend an ear to your partner. Find ten minutes at the end of the day to catch up on what happened in the other partner's day. Find time away from work, kids, other family to sit down and have an open and honest conversation. Go out on a date. Remember, listening to your partner, and being able to talk openly, is a critical part of the START-NOW program.

Flexibility in the Marriage

To make a marriage work, it is important to be flexible. Life doesn't always go according to plan. Be ready to adjust when things go wrong in your relationship — and they will!

What makes a marriage successful is the willingness of both partners to work together to overcome the problems that will inevitably arise.

If you think you can change your partner, think again. The truth is that most of the time you can't. Learn to accept your partner as he or she is, and stop trying to change them. Take the good with the bad.

Having a Family

Psychological trauma can have an impact on the family you create with your partner. Many people who have had a traumatic childhood are hesitant to have kids of their own, because they don't want to bring children into a cruel world, or they don't want to take the chance that their children will suffer. Maybe they feel they don't have a good handle on their emotions, or that, because of learned patterns from childhood, they may perpetuate the abuse they experienced as children onto their own children.

The fact that you are reading this book means you're trying to make things better for yourself and your family. Having a child can be a truly enriching and rewarding experience for survivors of psychological trauma. In our experience people with a history of psychological trauma who are actively trying to understand the impact of that trauma on themselves and others and who are doing the kinds of things we advocate in this book can make great parents. They often have a sort of a-ha moment where they realize that raising kids is not a pain in the ass, as they may have been led to believe in their family of origin, but is instead a rich source of meaning, love, and connection. Also, your recovery from your trauma history will give you insights and experience that you can teach to your children. One thing is for sure, your kid's childhoods probably won't be as bad as yours was!

In summary, we encourage you to strongly consider having a family, if there is a part of you who wants children. You do need to be mindful about how your trauma impacts your ability to work together with your partner as co-parents so that you can head off any problems.

Traps and Pitfalls in the Marriage Relationship

There are a number of traps people can fall into in a marriage, and some of them are specific to couples where one or both partners are affected by psychological trauma:

- One trap people get into is thinking that they will "fix" their partner after they marry them. Maybe the person is abusive or an alcoholic. Maybe you used wishful thinking, with the idea that marriage will help your partner "settle down." People rarely change, and if they do it is done because they want to (and not just because they want to stay married). So go into a marriage or a committed relationship with the attitude that what you see is what you get.

- Another way people try to fix their marriage is by having kids. Maybe you think your partner will change with kids in his or her life. You shouldn't have kids for any other reason than to love and raise them. When kids come into the world carrying baggage with them, or have an agenda placed on them, family relationships get out of kilter. You shouldn't have kids to fill a need in yourself, or to fix something that is wrong with your partner.

- Maybe your partner is a trauma victim, and you want to fill the "void" or rescue them. Or maybe you are the wounded one, looking for someone to throw you a lifeline. Intimate relationships do have a healing effect on traumatized people, but it shouldn't be the only reason to get married. You need a solid foundation of love and mutual respect.

Accepting the fact that you cannot change your partner doesn't mean that you should let them stagnate on their path toward recovery from psychological trauma. You will have to learn to differentiate between the trauma-related attitudes and behaviors, which can change, and the inherent parts of their personality that you won't be able to change. You will have to be patient in joining them on their journey to recovery, and avoid the "just get over it" or "snap out of it" language we argue against in so many parts of this book.

Here's another trap: I am going to stay in the marriage no matter what. That's like tying yourself to the mast for the entire journey of life. Where do you get that belief? Is it your church, or your family? If you look closely, you'll find that the people who are giving you that message aren't doing so well themselves.

Don't think that simply because the two of you share a faith (Christian, Jewish, Muslim, Buddhist, etc.), your marriage will be safe. This simpy isn't so, largely because many don't practice what they preach.

The fact is that if the couple allows the marriage to go stale, no belief system or set of moral values is going to save it. Sooner or later, the couple will most likely break up. The alternative is to live together in misery, which isn't a good choice. Maybe you're concerned about the kids. The fact is if you are fighting a lot, your kids might be relieved to have you break up. Is it economics? Going out on your own may be just what you need to break out of a stagnant and sterile rut, and to acquire some badly needed confidence through taking on new challenges successfully.

Another trap is making everything else, including your marriage, take a back seat to your children. If the couple isn't getting along, they won't be effective parents, anyway. If one or both parents puts all of their attention on the kids, the kids will think it is weird and feel uncomfortable, even if they don't tell you directly.

Putting too much emphasis on the kids may be an unconscious attempt to avoid the elephant in the room, which is the psychological trauma that one of the partners was exposed to. You will be better parents to your children if you are a strong and effective couple. You need to support each others' needs as adults to have the right mental state to be great parents. Rather than waste your energy on these kinds of behaviors, like over-prioritizing your kids, focus instead on the more productive task of following the points in the START-NOW program.

Sexual Relations are an Important Part of Intimacy

A lot of times with work, kids, financial strains, and other priorities, the couple's sex life can go on the back burner. It's easy to take one's partner for granted.

Or sometimes anger builds, and that interferes with having sex, which makes the cycle get worse. The anger may originally have been linked to the psychological trauma, but once it gets into the relationship, it takes on a life of its own.

One or the other of the couple may think that sex is not important, or they may have a low libido. A history of childhood sexual abuse may make the affected partner anxious or fearful during sex, or it may make them have flashbacks.

Medical or psychiatric problems can also interfere.

An active sex life, however, is a critical part of any relationship. It is the glue that holds the relationship together. If there are issues with your sex life, it is important to address these issues directly, and not try to avoid them, or hope they'll go away, or that the other person won't notice.

Medications used for the treatment of trauma-related mental disorders, like the SSRI type antidepressants, can decrease libido. It is important to talk to your doctor to and find out if there are possible medical reasons that are interfering with your sex life.

If that doesn't work, you should find a marital counselor whom both of you can talk to and get everything out into the open. Sunlight is the best disinfectant, and it's important to discuss everything with the help of a professional, even if it can feel awkward or strange.

Keep Lines of Communication Open

Having an open line of communication is critical in a marriage. Figure out what you want to communicate to your partner, and listen, listen, listen. Make an appointment to talk to your partner some time when you are not stressed or tired or in a bad mood.

Decide in advance what you want from the conversation. Say things that support the conversation, rather than cutting it off. Stay away from judgmental statements, like "you did this" or "if you do that again I'm going to leave you." Often just repeating back what the other person said to make sure you understand what they are trying to communicate is the best way to go.

Instead of saying this...	Say this...
I hate it when you ignore me.	When you ignore me it makes me feel bad (unloved, empty, anxious)
Stop tuning me out!	When I feel like you are not listening to me, it makes me feel unhappy
What the hell are you talking about?	Let me try and rephrase what you are saying, I think you are trying to say...
Get off the couch and take out the garbage!	Let's sit down and discuss what needs to be done around the house and how we are going to divide up the tasks.
You don't understand me!	When I feel like you are not listening to me it makes me feel bad.
You're such a self-centered jerk.	When I feel like you aren't taking me into the equation it makes me feel lonely.

FIGURE 19: CHANGING YOUR CONVERSATION

Be open about what's bothering you, but do it in a respectful way. Say things like "when you do x I feel y" rather than "stop tuning me out!" Check in with your partner to see if you were heard. Rephrase what your partner told you. When you rephrase things, it shows that you are listening to what the other person is trying to say. It's also a good way to defuse a situation, and slow things down if things are getting tense. People always feel supported when you rephrase what they say, because it makes them feel heard. Mirroring back what you hear is a good communication technique that you will never go wrong using. When you communicate, make sure you have your partner's undivided attention. Answer appropriately to questions.

Focus on improving communication with your partner:

- Identify what you need out of the relationship.

- Check in to find out if your partner understands your needs.

- Identify when you feel alone and unsupported, and why.

- Resolve conflict firmly and directly. Don't use techniques like total avoidance, or overt aggression, violence or hostility. These approaches don't work in the long run.

- Touch base during the day via email, text, messaging or Skype. Maintaining that connection will help the intimacy in your relationship grow. That will make both of you happier.

A lot of couples feel it's inevitable they'll get into arguments. It's true that all couples fight sooner or later, but an argument doesn't have to be the end of the world. There are things you can do to turn it around.

But first let's try and identify what is going on in your relationship:

- How often do you have fights?

- What do you fight about most often with your partner?

- How do you make up?

- How long do either of you stay mad?

- When you fight are you making accusations against your partner?

- Do you use negative comments and put-downs?

Don't become a martyr or victim in your relationship. On the other hand, don't become a bully to your partner. Putting the other person down, or allowing yourself to be put down, will never get you what you want. It will just put the other person on the defensive. What do you think you will achieve by yelling or making derogatory or down-putting remarks? Try and turn your putdowns into re-phrasing. Make "you are a jerk" into "when you act that way it makes me feel sad/angry/lonely/etc." Avoid using "you" and use "I" instead.

Stay focused on the goal of resolving conflict. Make compromises you can live with.

Learn how to say "I'm sorry."

Resolving Parenting Issues

One of the biggest causes of stress and conflict in marriages are arguments about how to raise the children. It is important that a couple agrees on how to parent their kids. The children need to see you approach them as a team, otherwise they will figure out ways to wiggle through the rules and go around you...and do even more to set you against your spouse.

Meet with your spouse apart from your children and agree on what kind of rules and boundaries you want for your children. You are not always going to have complete agreement, but these differences of opinion need to be ironed out away from the children. They should not be witnesses to a public debate about what is the best way to set limits for them.

Don't ally with your kids against your partner. Use time-outs rather than physical violence. Make sure to tell your kids when they are doing something you like. Kids need to hear positive things from you as well as get feedback when they are doing something wrong. You might have to remind yourself to do this on a regular basis.

Just as important for your kids as for your relationships is spending time with your spouse alone and away from the kids. Make an appointment or a date. Doing fun things with your partner is a way of bonding and growing more intimate. Make a "date night out." Use family and friends as baby-sitters to get some time alone. Write your spouse into your schedule. Use the time to talk, the T in the START program.

Money is a Major Source of Stress in Marriages

Together with kids, money is the major wrecker of marriages. What roles do you and your partner have related to money? Who is the spender? Who is the saver? Are both partners aware of the financial situation? If one spouse has been handling all of the financial issues, when that spouse dies, the other person can become completely lost.

Find a way to compromise so both partners feel satisfied with the approach to finances. Make financial decisions as a team.

Bottom Line on Working Together as Couples

In summary, keep all lines of communication open. Learn how to work within the couple as partners. Watch out for critical issues around raising children and money that can bring a marriage down. Stay committed and monogamous if you want to have a foundation of trust.

Have fun together, talk to each other, and spend time alone as a couple. Go out on dates, and talk. Take pride on how you are collaborating on the path toward real recovery from psychological trauma. Pay attention to financial planning. Work as partners in parenting your kids. When all else fails, say you're sorry.

And don't forget to work together as you follow the points of the START-NOW program.

CHAPTER 14: MILITARY FAMILIES — UNIQUE ROLES

Military families deal with a number of unique issues. However, a number of these issues have similarities to other families affected by psychological trauma. So read on if you are in a military family or know someone who is, or if you want to pick up some tips that may help you with your family.

FIGURE 20: COMBAT DEPLOYMENT CAN EXERT A HEAVY TOLL ON THE SOLDIER AND THE FAMILY

Combat Deployment and the Family

One thing military families usually have in common is that a parent and spouse has deployed to a foreign combat zone, most recently Iraq or Afghanistan. In today's military, families often have two, three, or four or more deployments, which is a significant change from the past.

We say the families deploy, because when the soldier deploys, it affects the whole family.

Understanding the psychological effects of deployment and combat trauma on the family are important to helping the family cope as a whole. These observations are based on our experiences with a ten-day intensive program we developed for military families at the Callaway Gardens in Pine Mountain, Georgia, which we talk more about below.

The Wars in Iraq and Afghanistan

At the peak of the war in Iraq and Afghanistan—Operation Iraqi Freedom/Operation Enduring Freedom (OIF/OEF)–over 150,000 soldiers were deployed each year to the combat zone, and 12%-17% of them developed PTSD. In the State of Georgia alone, up to 13,000 soldiers returned each year from Iraq and Afghanistan. There were an equal number of direct family members in Georgia with a deployed spouse or parent in this time period. Many returning soldiers have been afflicted with a wide range of physical and mental health complaints.

Effects of Combat Deployment on Physical and Mental Health

Less than 40% of returning soldiers from OIF with PTSD will seek treatment for their disorder.

These military personnel will suffer from loss of work productivity, use more health care resources and have higher rates of disease, including cardiovascular disease (CVD), diabetes, asthma, PTSD and depression. Military personnel deployed in violent combat arenas have increased rates of impulsive and risk taking behavior, as well as increased violence and aggression upon returning from deployment, compared to non-deployed military personnel. They also have more physical symptoms, mental health problems, and alcohold and substance abuse.

Most alarming are the statistics related to the rise of suicide. The number of suicides in active duty military personnel and reserves increased from 160 in 2001 to 309 in 2009. The number of completed suicides was even higher in 2010, according to the Department of Defense.

In our opinion an important factor that contributes to suicide is a sense of anger and alienation upon return from combat deployments when they have difficulty in re-integrating into their communities and families. That's why in working with military families we always focus on family first.

The Cost of Deployment-related Mental Health Problems

Not addressing the consequences of stress related to deployment to combat zones is associated with significant costs. Among veterans of the Vietnam war, 23% percent of those with PTSD were not working in the years after returning from deployment, compared to 4% percent without PTSD.

The cost of lost productivity based on a rate of PTSD of 15% in the three million veterans who served in Vietnam and had an average salary of $30,000 over forty years is thus over $3.6 trillion dollars.

A RAND report from 2008 ("Stop loss: A nation weighs the tangible consequences of invisible combat wounds.") estimated the two-year year cost of PTSD and depression in terms of treatment, lost productivity and loss of life due to suicide in 1.6 million soldiers returning from Iraq and Afghanistan at $4-6.2 billion depending on how suicides are accounted for.

Individual costs per service member are

- $10,298 for PTSD,

- $16,884 for co-morbid PTSD and depression, and

- $25,757 for depression.

Furthermore, $1.7 billion ($2306 per case of PTSD, $2997 for PTSD/depression, and $9240 for depression) could be saved by treating all service members with these conditions. Extrapolated over forty years of additional lifetime, assuming that these conditions become chronic in half of persons, the dollar amount would be over $40 billion.

Effects of Combat Deployment on Military Families

The families of returning soldiers are also affected by their war time experiences.

Studies have shown that the families of veterans with combat-related PTSD exhibit more adjustment problems than the families of combat veterans who do not develop PTSD.

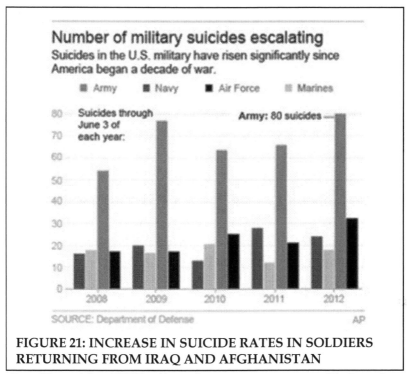

FIGURE 21: INCREASE IN SUICIDE RATES IN SOLDIERS RETURNING FROM IRAQ AND AFGHANISTAN

Families with a PTSD affected veteran were more likely to be rated as high

- on a Marital Problems Index (49% versus 9%),

- Parental Problem Index (55% versus 17%), and

- family adjustment (extreme) (55% versus 19%).

**FIGURE 22: THE SOLDIER
RETURNS HOME**

The rates of mental disorders in spouses who remain stateside are similar to those of their spouses deployed in a combat zone. Divorce rates have increased from 2.6% in 2001 to 3.6% in 2009 in military families, according to the Department of Defense. Children with deployed parents compared to those with non-deployed military parents suffer men tal disorders at the rate of 20% versus 16% for boys, and 16% versus 14% for girls.

A Program for Re-integration of Soldiers into Family and Community

Soldiers are prepared by the military for deployment, but not necessarily for their return from the combat zone. Combat zones are associated with high stress, high physical demands, high adrenaline, high leadership and a high level of job sophistication.

Return from deployment feels like a rapid deceleration for soldiers, with an associated relative lack of activity, and if they are discharged from active duty service, possibly no job. Some soldiers are not ready for the return home and post-deployment period. Multiple forces converge that threaten connection with the soldier's family, work, and environment.

We decided that a program was needed for soldiers when they return from deployment, where they could spend time with their families in a relaxed outdoor environment, and learn about stress and gain additional skills related to diet, health, and relationships, as well as reconnect with their families, peers, and the natural environment.

In April and July of 2012, our research program at the Emory University School of Medicine, in conjunction with the US Army Maneuver Center of Excellence at Fort Benning in Columbus, Georgia, the Callaway family (Edward and Bo Callaway) and the Callaway Gardens Foundation conducted two ten-day pilot programs at the Callaway Gardens for soldiers returning from Iraq and Afghanistan and their families. The program was designed to facilitate re-integration of soldiers into their families, their communities, nature, and with each other. We called our program the Callaway Homecoming Initiative (CHI).

The mission of CHI was to help returning soldiers and their families learn about the symptoms of stress and the transition from the combat theater, become educated about health, diet, exercise, relationships, and personal life skills, adjust to life at home, and re-connect with nature, peers and family.

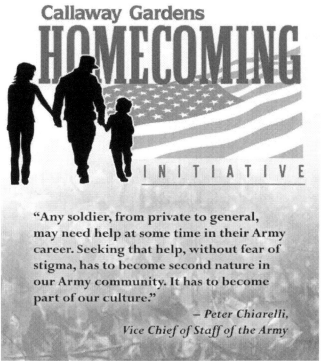

**FIGURE 23: CALLAWAY HOMECOMING
INITIATIVE (CHI) PROGRAM BROCHURE**

Program for soldiers returning from
Iraq and Afghanistan and their
families, 2012. Copyright © 2012
Callaway Gardens, used by
permission of Callaway Gardens.

This was done through a ten-day residential period for soldiers
who had just returned from deployment and their immediate families
in the environment of the Callaway Gardens, a 10,000-acre complex
with cabins for the families, gardens, a nature center, golf, tennis and
sailing, and a variety of family-oriented activities like ziplines and
organized team competitions.

We included married soldiers who recently returned from
deployment to a combat zone. We found that facilitating the coming

together of families in an environment where individual family members can share their experiences with each other and their peers who can

relate to their similar experiences was very helpful in promoting the re-integration of service members into their families and communities.

Our experience with this program was highly positive, with one spouse telling us that her soldier husband and she had decided to divorce, but changed their minds after going through the program.

This program helped not only the soldier, but also the spouse and children who were spared the devastating break-up of the family. Much of the material in this book is derived from the series of lectures given to soldiers and their families in the CHI program.

In this chapter we present some of the material that was offered in lectures called "Military Families" to the families during CHI, both the spouses alone, the soldiers alone, and the two together as couples. We also present some of what we learned during the question and answer sessions that followed with the spouses and the soldiers.

Other material from the CHI lectures is incorporated into other chapters of this book, including Working Together as Couples (Chapter 13), Better Lifestyles (Chapter 12), and Tools for Coping with Stress (Chapter 11).

Soldiers and their families go through multiple psychological stages before, during, and after deployment to a combat zone. These stages include:

- pre-deployment (the month or so before leaving),

- initial deployment (the first month in the combat zone),

- sustainment (the middle portion of deployment),

- re-deployment (two months before return), and

- the post-deployment period.

The Phases of Deployment

1. Pre-deployment

The pre-deployment period represents the time leading up to deployment.

The soldier may seem "already deployed" since he is focused on his unit and getting ready. There is an endless "to do" list before the soldier deploys.

It is not uncommon to have a "big argument" with the spouse — more likely related to stress than fundamental problems in the marriage. But the soldier may deploy before there is time to make up and come to a mutual understanding.

In general, there may not be a chance to tie up loose ends. Kids are getting ready for the adjustment of not having two parents in the house, and worried about what will happen to their soldier/parent.

Some spouses admit that there is so much tension leading up to "the time" when the soldier actually leaves that they almost feel a sense of relief when it's over. Many spouses we met with in our groups admitted this and felt relieved that others felt the same way, since they had not talked about it before because they felt guilty.

2. Deployment

The deployment period refers to the first month of deployment overseas.

Spouses at home may have trouble adjusting to not having the spouse in bed, or someone around the house to help out. They have to get used to being single parents. The kids need to adjust to not having an extra parent.

Many military spouses seem to learn to do a number of things that non-military spouses don't do; for example, it might be typical that one spouse controls the finances and pays the bills, while the other one doesn't know anything about it. Military families don't have this luxury, so they evolve as two parallel units that are both self-sufficient. This may be associated with its own problems.

3. Sustainment

Sustainment refers to the period when everyone settles into the routine of the soldier being away from home for a long period of time, i.e., the months in the middle of the deployment, after the soldier and family have gotten used to him or her not being there, and before they start psychologically getting ready for their return a couple of months before the end of the deployment period.

During this period, the spouse on the home front goes through a period of endlessly waiting for the phone to ring – a never-ending dread by the spouse and the kids that they will get the phone call, or the visit to the door, telling them that their parent and spouse has been killed in combat.

**FIGURE 24: AN
INCREASING NUMBER
OF OUR MILITARY
ARE WOMEN**

Some spouses report sleeping with their cell phones on their chest, because they never know when the call will come in, day or night, and they may not get the chance to call back.

Sometimes when the call does come, it can be frustrating, because they have to drop everything they are doing to attend to the soldier. They may feel like there is no appreciation for the fact that they have their own life that is not less important than what is happening in the combat zone.

Sometimes well-intentioned efforts to support military families can backfire and themselves become the source of stress. The Family Readiness Groups (FRGs) are networks of spouses with soldiers in the same unit that were formed with the goal of providing mutual support. However, rumors can quickly spread.

When there is a casualty or the unit goes out on a combat mission, there is a blackout of information for security reasons. During the period (which may be up to two days) the spouses cannot communicate with their partners. In this environment rumors can spread. We have met at least one spouse who thought that her partner was killed in action based on rumors in the FRG, when in fact her spouse was unharmed.

Rumors can also spread about infidelity and other issues. For these reasons, rumors should be brought out into the open as soon as possible so that they can be quelled.

4. Re-deployment

The re-deployment period refers to the month or two before the soldier returns home.

This an adjustment period both for the soldier and for the family members on the home front. The spouse may panic over the list of things to do to prepare for the return of the soldiers.

Sometimes the spouse may not "be ready" for the return of the soldier.

5. Post-deployment

Post-deployment starts with the initial joy and anxiety of re-unitement—most couples and their children report great joy at the initial reunion.

Once the soldier is back in the house, however, it may take time to adjust. Sometimes the soldier wants to indulge his kids, or introduces changes in the rules for the kids which frustrates the other spouse who has been holding to boundaries about things like bedtime or video time.

The spouse may have to get used to having someone else in the house. The new parent may have his or her own ideas of discipline for the kids. It may take some time to adjust.

Small children may experience some fear at seeing a parent they don't remember. Often small children see their deployed parent as someone who lives in the computer, since their contact with them up to that point has been through Skype or the telephone. Some of the families in our program printed out life-size full-length photographs of the deployed parent and made "cardboard cut-out daddies" to help the kids have something to represent the missing parent.

When that parent returns and wants them to sit on their laps, it can be a little scary at first and may require some period for adjustment.

Coming Home

When a soldier comes back from the combat front, s/he can't just

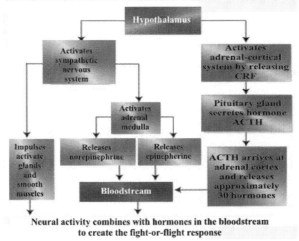

NEURAL ACTIVITY IN THE FIGHT-OR-FLIGHT RESPONSE

Neural activity combines with hormones in the bloodstream
to create the fight-or-flight response

**FIGURE 25: NEUROPHYSIOLOGIC ACTIVITY
IN THE FIGHT OR FLIGHT RESPONSE**

"turn off" their combat frame of mind the way you flick a switch to turn off the light. Soldiers in a combat zone have a heightened responsiveness and increased vigilance.

Being hyped up and on guard is a normal and adaptive response to being in a combat zone. If you weren't on your toes all the time, you might be the one to get picked off by a sniper or to not respond fast enough to an ambush. In that case, you might be coming back in a body bag instead of an airplane.

You've got to be ready to stand and fight or get away quick, something we call the "fight or flight response." And you've got to decide what to do right away — there isn't time to waste.

As discussed earlier in this book, stress hormones adrenaline and cortisol help with the fight or flight response. They pour into the body when there is a threat and cause an increase in heart rate, blood pressure, and breathing rate, and shunt energy to the muscles and brain so you think fast, run fast, and fight hard.

Since the combat mode is an automatic response (if you had to think too much about it, you probably wouldn't survive) it isn't something you can just "will" to go away.

That's why soldier's families shouldn't be impatient if their soldiers are jumpy or on guard when they get back from the war zone, and that their jumpiness doesn't go away right away.

THE PHYSIOLOGY OF FIGHT OR FLIGHT

What we know is happening...

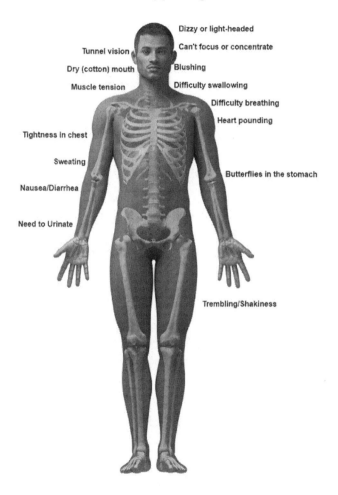

FIGURE 26: THE PHYSIOLOGY OF FLIGHT OR FIGHT

Learned Combat-Zone Behaviors Don't Translate Well to Civilian Life

Soldiers learn other behaviors to adapt in a combat zone that may seem strange after they come home.

In Iraq, soldiers drove their armored vehicles at full bore down the middle of the road. If there were some vehicles in front of them, they would pass like maniacs, even if it meant putting everyone at risk. They did that because explosive devices were left at the side of the road in garbage bags or other hidden places.

These "improvised explosive devices" (or IEDs) were detonated remotely by insurgents when the soldiers were on patrol. If they got slowed down by other vehicles or by crowds of civilians in the road, they became easy targets for IEDs. That's why they learned how to drive fast and furious when they were on patrol.

Back home, a simple drive to the grocery store can become a frightening experience. They also can drive other people crazy — they'll often honk at little old ladies who they think are driving too slow or getting in the way. Seeing a bag of garbage on the side of the road can cause them to swerve.

Although this may drive you crazy — your own trauma — you have to understand that this comes from their experiences in a combat zone, and it may take a while to go away.

When the Combat Mind Interferes with Living

The difficulty in turning off the combat mind set may come out in other ways:

- Soldiers may stay at home to avoid things that trigger memories of combat. They may feel safer.

- They may get anxious when their loved ones go out as well.

- They may jump at loud noises.

- Sleeping with someone else in bed may feel strange.

- Being a parent, and making decisions will be a challenge.

- For many soldiers, it is the first time out of the military, and they must learn how to get a job, balance a checkbook, shop for groceries, cook for themselves (instead of eating on base), clean the house, and be a parent.

- Wives and kids must adjust to having another person in the house.

The Callaway Homecoming Initiative (CHI)

The Callaway Homecoming Initiative (CHI) was focused on reintegrating soldiers with their families.

For the first few days of the program, soldiers came in by themselves. In the mornings, they got a series of lectures from mental health experts on mental and physical health, relationships, better lifestyles and transitioning from the combat theater. Afternoons were spent in team building activities.

After several days, we brought in the families, and had a lecture on unique role of military spouses just for the spouses, followed by a group discussion and a team building activity in the afternoon. The next day we gave lectures to the couples on working together as couples, and did similar things for the kids.

The program let soldiers spend time with their spouses and children in a setting that allowed them to learn and grow together, have positive shared experiences, and participate in activities that allowed them to reconnect with nature and bond together as families.

The lessons we learned from the program apply to all families where one or more people is affected by psychological trauma. We learned that one of the most important factors in the recovery from psychological trauma is the love and support of the family members. When soldiers, or anyone for that matter, become detached from their families, it leads to anger, isolation, despair, and ultimately suicide.

In recognition of the important role of family members, we have written the next chapter for the significant others and spouses of those affected by psychological trauma.

CHAPTER 15: INVOLVING FRIENDS AND FAMILY IN YOUR RECOVERY

This chapter is for the friends and families of the person who has been affected by psychological trauma. We outline here some strategies you can you to help your loved one in the recovery process. We also discuss what to do if you suspect your loved one has experienced a trauma, but you don't know for sure.

Psychological trauma affects not only the people who experienced the trauma, but everyone in their sphere as well. Sexual trauma can affect intimate relationships, and all traumas influence the sense of connectedness and emotional attachment between trauma victims and their family members.

We talked about couples in the earlier chapter on working together as couples. Here we talk about what you as the friend or family member of a traumatized person can do to help them.

How To Recognize the Traumatized Person

How do you know if your friend or partner has been traumatized, and if it is now affecting his or her life?

There are certain signs, certain patterns of behavior, that will give you a clue. As we touched on in an earlier chapter, the behaviors can include:

- becoming angry for little or no reason,

- becoming emotionally withdrawn or distant,

- always wanting to sit with your back against the wall,

- feeling very anxious or frightened when there is a reminder of the trauma.

- alcohol or substance abuse that is out of control

- being jumpy or easily startled

- outbursts of anger that seem to have no reason or justification

How to Help the Trauma Victim

To help, you, the partner of the trauma victim, first need to know as much as possible about the trauma. You should not let the defensiveness of the trauma survivor hold you back.

That said, there is a time and place for everything. You need to be patient and let the survivor talk about it in his own time and place. Just talking about it will be beneficial.

The trauma survivor may need to go back and get more information about the past. This may involve confronting difficult relatives or being exposed to reminders of events that are very painful and may make them feel worse.

You can play an important role as a support and as someone who can give external validation and a sense of reality outside the view of family members who may have imposed ideas on the survivor that have resulted in distorted memories and viewpoints.

You can read and follow the points of the START-NOW program so that you can help your loved one on their path to recovery from psychological trauma.

Recovery is Never an Easy Road

One thing you should be aware of is that the process of recovery from psychological trauma is not quick or easy. It is best to stay away from language like "just get over it," or "just move on with your life," or "focus on me right now in the present instead of living in the past," or "why don't you focus on the living instead of the dead?" That kind of language leaves trauma survivors feeling hopeless and inadequate, because the truth is that they may have tried to do this in the past and have been unsuccessful, for the simple reason that IT DOESN'T WORK!

Why should you spend a lot of time on something that will be frustrating and annoying for both of you and that won't get you the result you want, anyway? Why indeed?

You Are a Critical Part of Your Loved One's Recovery

The good news is that you are in fact central to the recovery process of your loved one, even if it will be a long haul. Trauma victims often become detached from people close to them, emotionally numb and cut off. They wall off their feelings related to the trauma. This has the effect of numbing out all feelings, since it isn't possible to selectively isolate the bad ones.

If they do this, it may make you feel as though they don't care about you, love you, or want to be intimate with you. This is not, however, a conscious decision that can be "willed" away. Emotional detachment and numbing is a symptom of PTSD. They can't always help it.

The fact is that they need a connection with another person or persons to keep from feeling isolated and alone or from thinking the world is an evil place. This alienation from friends and family leads to only one place: depression, alcohol and drug abuse, and ultimately despair that could lead to suicide.

The main focus of our program for military families, described in the last chapter, is putting the emphasis on the entire family to help the person affected by psychological trauma, in this case soldiers returning from Iraq. We do this because it not only helps the family, it also helps the veteran.

So what do you do?

The first thing is to read up on the START-NOW program outlined in later chapters, which we will briefly introduce here.

Working with the START-NOW Program

Working with the START-NOW program is a critical part of helping your loved one on the path toward recovery from psychological trauma.

The first and foremost step, and the one that needs you, is the S part of START, which is Seek Safety and Support. Survivors need to be able to go to you and get support as they start on their journey toward recovery from psychological trauma. This will not be an easy process, as they will have to re-visit (the "R" in START) the trauma mentally, emotionally, and physically (to return to where the trauma took place).

The next important step which involves you is to Talk about their psychological trauma, and for you to listen in a non-judgmental way. They need to talk and be heard by you, and to get validation and love from you as worthwhile human beings who deserve love and respect.

This process, however, cannot be rushed. You shouldn't pressure your loved one to dump or pour out their thoughts and feelings. Rather, you should be there, available and ready to listen when they are ready to talk.

Dealing with Anniversary Reactions

Another thing you should be aware of is that your loved one may have what we call "anniversary reactions."

Anniversary reactions are very common. As we discussed earlier in this book, they involve a return of the thoughts and feelings associated with the original trauma on the specific date that the trauma occurred. The reactions may come on slowly, as the trauma survivor reacts <u>unconsciously</u> to subtle cues, like the change in the season.

Trauma survivors may become emotionally withdrawn, or more irritable and depressed than usual, but not be aware of it or know why these things are happening.

The best thing is to prepare for the anniversary. Know that things may be rough for a couple of weeks. If the trauma survivor withdraws, understand that it is not a rejection of you, but a necessary, and temporary, retreat from the memory of the events. Also be prepared for stronger emotional reactions to everyday events around this time period.

Is it Me or the Trauma?

Another confusing part about being in a relationship with a trauma survivor is sorting out the difference between behavior that is the result of the survivor's trauma, and problems that are specific to your relationship. Many times the two areas will overlap and intertwine.

Reading the chapter in this book on working together as couples (Chapter 13) is a good place to start to make headway in this area. You may also need to seek help with a couples therapist who has experience in dealing with these kind of issues, and can help you sort through things.

It is important to educate yourself about psychological trauma so that you can help your loved one as much as possible. Often, just knowing that something is "the PTSD" rather than "you" or "them" can go a long way toward easing the tension and making the situation better.

So read on in this book and learn as much as you can about the effects of psychological trauma, and how you can help your loved one on the road to recovery.

The best to start it, of course, our START-NOW program, which we discuss in the next chapter.

CHAPTER 16: THE START PROGRAM

By now, you probably realize that you won't be able to recover from your trauma by sitting and waiting, or hoping that it will go away by itself. You also probably realize by now that it doesn't work to try and cope with it through drugs or alcohol, sex addictions, having an email or a physical affair, becoming a workaholic, or other ways you try to distract yourself to keep your trauma at arm's length.

FIGURE 27: ARE YOU READY TO START?

And all that worthless advice from friends and family to move, get over it, put it behind you, is just that...worthless. That's because you can't "put it behind you."

You need to take an active approach toward dealing with your trauma. It isn't easy, and it isn't quick, but one thing it's NOT is impossible.

How to Work the START-NOW Program

We have come up with a way to remember the most important parts of your path toward healing from psychological trauma called START-NOW. You can combine it with tools for coping with stress and better lifestyles as part of a comprehensive program for recovery from psychological trauma.

You should start with the first letters of the START-NOW program and move through them to the end. But you shouldn't view this as like a journey on a train that goes from one stop to the next, and never goes backward. It is a journey, but many times you will return to the first letters of START-NOW — your building blocks — and re-do your lessons before you head back down the road on your journey.

Instead of a linear trip, it is best to think of the START-NOW program as more like peeling an onion. You will go all the way through the program, and then when you get down to a deeper level of your trauma, you will want to start again to make sure your foundation is solid before you revisit things with new eyes.

Sometimes following the points of the program will trigger your fight or flight response, and you will need to re-read the chapter on tools for coping with stress (Chapter 11), or you will need to focus on exercise, as described in better lifestyles (Chapter 12), to burn off the energy generated by the process.

If your emotions impact your relationship, re-read the chapter on working together as couples (Chapter 13). But above all, know that you are making positive, forward progress on your path toward real recovery from psychological trauma. It won't happen quickly, and things won't move in a linear direction, but in the end you will be glad you made the effort, and your loved ones will be glad, too.

We call our program the START-NOW program for a number of reasons.

For one, we think you should — you guessed it — start now to recover from your psychological trauma because there is no better time to do so. There never is a "good time" to start grappling with your demons, just like there never is a "good time" to quit smoking, or to start exercising.

The fact that you have gotten this far in reading this book shows that you have the motivation and the desire to take on this task. This is the perfect time.

One of the things the S in START-NOW stands for is...Start now.

S is for Start Now and Seek Safety and Support

Start the START NOW program. Start adopting better lifestyles. Start using tools to cope with stress.

S also stands for Stop; namely, stop abusing drugs and alcohol, stop self-destructive, unhealthy, and addictive behaviors, stop doing things that will have a negative impact on your mental health, stop destroying your relationships, and stop the negative downward spiral that will lead to only one place, which is isolation, depression, suicide and death.

S, in addition to standing for Start now, also stands for Seek Safety and Support. It is also good sometimes to have Silence, which we will talk about in more detail below.

If you got a blister from a tight fitting shoe would you put it on again? Of course not. You want to remove your foot from the thing that is causing the injury. If you don't do that, it won't be able to heal. In the same way, the first thing you have to do is create boundaries between yourself and those who have hurt you in the past. Otherwise you won't be able to start the healing process.

An important part of seeking safety is to know how to protect yourself. Psychological trauma can expose you and make you vulnerable to further victimization. There will be people who claim they are trying to help you, but who are in fact serving their own interests or trying to use you.

Con artists, charlatans and cult leaders, have an intuitive sense for vulnerable people. This unfortunately can include survivors of psychological trauma, who have not successfully made the journey of recovery, and whose self defense mechanisms are impaired. These con artists actually seek people out they think they can exploit.

Maybe you are reeling from a divorce or a split with your family, or are overwhelmed with your memories of your psychological trauma. They will try to make you think they're your friend, but they are not. They are like a wolf in sheep's clothing. They may end up taking more from you and hurting you, increasing your sense of isolation, anger and cynicism.

You are under no obligation to share your trauma with other people you do not feel safe with. Talking about your trauma is like opening an unhealed wound. If someone encourages you to talk about your trauma, tells you to "get it out" or "come clean" or "you'll feel better if you talk about it with me" or similar language, tell them you don't feel comfortable talking about it right now, or that's personal. There is no law that says you have to talk about anything about yourself with any person at any time.

There will be a time and place to talk and a person to talk to, but the first step is to set up your boundaries and give yourself a place to start to heal.

In general we recommend talking to a professional counselor or mental health care provider first; they can guide you about when and where are the best times to start to disclose, and what are the best times. You also should talk with an intimate partner whom you trust and with whom you have a history.

Another related area is talking to the public. If you were involved in a high profile trauma you may be sought out by the media. You may feel drawn to talk about your story to journalists for a number of reasons. But remember, the job of these people is to sell newspapers. Sometimes they can make you look bad, or they can stir memories of the trauma or make you feel manipulated. It is completely OK for you to say "I have no comment at this time."

You also have to be careful in dealing with the judicial system. If you were the victim or abuse or rape, you may be asked to come back and testify against your perpetrator. Or you may have to testify about a car accident. It is important for the courts to do their job, and you are doing a great service by removing people from the general public who might have the potential to do more harm. But if you do have to testify or talk to lawyers and the police, make sure you give yourself plenty of leeway, both before and after the court date:

- know that your anxiety and trauma symptoms will increase leading up to the date,

- that it may take you weeks to recover, and

- understand that this is a normal part of the process, and the police and the attorneys have a lot of experience working with trauma survivors, and they can help you get through the process.

However, you will encounter some people in the judicial system who are not sensitive, and you will need to protect yourself from them. This may mean doing things like asking to take a break if you are being interviewed by an over-aggressive lawyer. Try to alert your friends and family about how these events will affect you in advance.

You also have to learn how to protect yourself from some of your friends, family, and co-workers. They may come under the guise of "helping" you, but actually may do more harm than good. These are the people who tell you to "just put it behind you" or "just snap out of it" or "move on, get over it." Studies have shown that people with a history of psychological trauma who are suffering from mental symptoms actually do worse with this kind of essentially negative "support" than if they were just left alone. They also tell you "you don't need a therapist" or "you don't need a support group."

People who give you the "get over it" line are wolves in sheep's clothing. Just like the people who urge you to "get it all out," they act like they are there for your own good, and if you resist them, you are not being nice or resisting help.

The fact is that only you know what is best for you. Don't let other people tell you what your feelings are. They are not their feelings, they are your feelings. Only you can feel them. These people who are trying to tell you how you "should" respond or feel have never been there themselves, so they don't know what they are talking about. Or if they have been there, they have responded by using some type of denial. By telling you to just "buck up," "pull yourself together," and "get over it," they are shoring up their own defense systems. You see, if they let you feel your feelings, they might have to feel their own, too.

Those people may also have been a part of the source of your original trauma, so they are hardly the people you should consider role models or look to for advice on your recovery. Even if they were not the perpetrators of your trauma, they may be family members who didn't do enough to protect you because of their own denial about what was going on—they they were too self-absorbed, or they were impaired by drug or alcohol abuse.

Remember to look out for Number One—that's you. You have to learn how to set boundaries. That means there will be situations where you have to withdraw from others to get your boundaries and equilibrium back. That's why we say Sometimes Silence is nice, another key part of the S in START NOW.

One way to find safety is to find a place that you can go where you will not be interrupted. Turn off your phone, your computer, and allow yourself your right to establish boundaries between yourself and others. Get away to the beach, or a cabin in the mountains. If you don't have any money, go to the public library. Public libraries are free, and if you live in a city, the chances are that you won't run into anyone you know.

No one has the right to judge you negatively for doing things to protect yourself. No one has the right to intrude upon your space whenever they want to. You should not sacrifice yourself.

If you can't get to a physical place of safety right away, find a place of mental safety you can go to for refuge. Think about a memory of being on the beach, or on a mountain. Imagine the picture in your mind. Use some of the techniques discussed in Chapter 11, Tools for Coping with

Stress, to help you out with this. A friend of mine told me that when he had to go through a series of depositions by lawyers after being accused (falsely) of slander, he imagined himself inside of a bubble that protected him. Be creative and come up with your own methods for finding a mental place of refuge.

Although we advocate protecting yourself from toxic people, that doesn't necessarily mean you should become a hermit. There will be persons and situations that are supportive and helpful. Your support group will have people you can count on, and talk to. This could include your wife, girlfriend, brother, sister, brother, father, the guy next door, your friend, your barber, or someone at work. Often peer groups of individuals, whether through group therapy or other venues that have been through similar experiences, can be helpful. These people can make you feel like you are not a freak because they have experienced similar things, and have had similar reactions and emotions. This is called "normalization."

Intimate relationships can also be a vehicle for healing from trauma. By opening up to another person in whom you have complete trust, it makes you feel less alone. Just being able to put things into words that you only experienced physically and emotionally itself has a healing value. Also, having loving support can give you the courage and strength to be able to look at painful memories, bit by bit.

Make sure that your significant other is being supportive through thoughtful listening and reflecting back to you what they hear you saying. If they criticize you or tell you to get over it, move on, or similar language, or look uncomfortable talking to you about painful things, that may be a signal to you not to put to much confidence in that person's ability to help you through your healing process. Remember, support that is negative, judgmental or critical is not support at all. It actually can be toxic, and is best avoided as much as possible.

T is for Talking and Translating Feelings into Words.

T is for Telling people whom you trust about your story and Talking about how you feel. We've provided a list of the emotions commonly felt by survivors of psychological trauma in Appendix A. Once you have established the network of people you can trust, it is important to start talking about what happened to you.

FIGURE 28: TALKING AND TELLING BUILD TRUST

Talk about your trauma. Tell people how you feel. Talking puts feelings into words and helps change how the trauma is encoded in your brain. It allows you to create your own story. It also allows people to see what is going on inside of you and give you support. People aren't mind readers. If you don't tell them what is in your head, how will they know? Talking also gives you the chance to find other people who have had similar experiences or thoughts and feelings. This is what we call in the psych biz "normalization" and is a great way to get away from that feeling that you are an alien and no one has ever experienced what you have or felt your feelings, or that no one can ever understand how you feel. Remember, being that alien has helped you in the past and it may be hard to break away from it, so give yourself a break. You may need to give it a couple of shots.

And remember, don't start talking until you are in a safe place with safe and supportive people.

Talking about your trauma is best done initially with a therapist or mental health professional. These people are trained to listen in a non-judgmental manner to all manner of uncomfortable material. They can also help you with distortions in thinking that often occur around traumatic events, and help you identify the emotions that are associated with the trauma.

<u>T</u> is also for <u>T</u>ranslating your feelings into words. When you put scary memories into words, it makes them concrete, something you can work with, rather than just the scary stuff of nightmares. You can formulate what happened to you and discuss it with other people.

It also usually helps to write down your experiences, which is sort of the corollary of talking. This is the <u>R</u> of <u>R</u>e-write your experiences that we talk about in more detail later.

When traumatized people turn their traumatic events into stories, start talking about them, it actually changes the brain. That is because the brain is wired to understand the world through stories.

By putting your trauma into words, you make it a story, with a beginning, middle and end. This alone can have healing powers. From the time of the *Iliad* when Homer told the story of the traumatized warrior, Achilles, and probably for eons before that when primitive people huddled around the fire at night, people have been using stories to convey the experience of the collective group and to help individual members of the group come back into the fold and create meaning out of the experiences after going through a traumatic situation.

A psychiatrist friend of mine named Jonathan Shay, M.D., wrote a book about the similarities between Achilles in the *Iliad* and Vietnam veterans with PTSD called *Achilles and Vietnam*. He thought Achilles had PTSD. You should check it out.

There are other ways you can <u>T</u>ranslate your trauma that involve a variety of art forms. You can use painting or sculpture. Art can be a wonderful way to express things that you cannot find words for. Even if you are not a great painter, it can still be a healing experience.

Do you play an instrument? That can be an excellent vehicle for the expression of your emotions, and better yet it doesn't hurt anyone else, in fact it makes them happy.

Do you write poetry? Try translating your feelings into words.

Others express themselves through acting or theater. Acting gives us the license to freely express our emotions. Good drama thrives on conflict, and trauma is by its nature filled with conflict. You can also bring this conflict into writing plays or screenplays. One of the great things about theater and cinema is that negative emotions we normally discourage people from expressing — like anger, disgust, shame, and many others — are actually encouraged in those arenas. It is a place where there is a collective agreement that anything goes.

Any screenwriter who is worth his or her salt knows that great screenplays need conflict. No one wants to watch a movie where the characters sit around and agree with each other all the time. They've got to want something badly, and someone wants the opposite. Then *whammo!* You've got conflict… and a great film.

I am a screenplay writer. Last year, we formed a production company, called Laughing Cow Productions, and made one of my screenplays into a movie. It is a feature-length comedy called *Inheritance, Italian Style.* When I write screenplays, I find creating conflict between characters is a great way to work through unresolved conflicts from my own life. Then it is no longer my problem or my unresolved conflict… now it's the characters' problem! And the more you sit back and watch them sweat, the better the movie gets.

In theater and film, since you are a performer, you don't have to take ownership of the emotions you express in performances. One little secret of the entertainment industry is that many great comics came from terrible childhoods.

<u>A</u> is for <u>A</u>cceptance, <u>A</u>ction and <u>A</u>ltruism

Once you have established your zone of safety and have spent some time expressing yourself, including the rage and shame that may underlie some of your feelings about what happened to you, it is time to start to <u>A</u>ccept what happened to you.

FIGURE 29: LEARN TO ACCEPT WHAT HAPPENED TO YOU

Although this is an important part of your trauma recovery, you shouldn't force yourself to accept what happened in an unnatural way, or allow others to brow beat your into it. The process of acceptance is a gradual one that evolves in layers. It is not a light switch that you can simply turn on when you get the urge.

What happened to you was not right, was not ideal, and maybe it was unlucky, but nothing you can do now will change it. The mind can go round and round the eternal question asked by Job, *why?* But this merry-go-round of the brain can end up making you feel like a gerbil running on a wheel. Bad things happen to good people. A lot of us will have something really terrible happen to us. Look around you, and see the stories of others, some of them similar to yours, some worse, some not so bad, but still bad.

Some people never have something really bad happen to them. That is just the way life is. You can call yourself unlucky if you want, or question why certain things happened to you and not to other people, but that won't help you on your path toward recovery from psychological trauma.

What about anger? After all, you've definitely got a right to be angry. So go ahead, be angry. You can roll up all your anger into a ball, and feed it and watch it grow, but that won't get you anywhere, either. It is appropriate to express your righteous anger, but do it in the context of therapy, or with the goal of growing through it.

The other side of anger is grief. Read books about grief listed at the end of this book, like *Daily Meditations on Grief*. Anger is one step in the grief process. It comes after denial, and before depression (see Page 80). Anger is just one step on the way of the grieving process. Maybe you are stuck on anger because you are not allowing yourself to grieve.

Are you afraid to go to the next part, which is depression? It's not so bad, as long as you don't get down on yourself too much about it.

We talk about allowing yourself to grieve, because grief is something that will follow a natural course, unless you do something to actively try to stop it. Holding up grief takes a lot of energy. Let it go and put your energy into following the points of the START-NOW program.

Part of acceptance is not only accepting that the traumatic event happened to you, but accepting yourself. Many traumatized people have a sense of guilt over things that happened, or feel bad about themselves. Maybe someone died, or maybe you blame yourself.

For rape victims, it is easy to fall into the trap propagated by society — "slut shaming":

- maybe you could have done something to prevent the rape,

- maybe you shouldn't have been alone by yourself,

- maybe you drank too much, or

- maybe you repeat the negative mantras you picked up from your perpetrator, or others who did not protect you.

Stay away from that line of thinking. You are not the one who is responsible for you being a victim, your perpetrator is.

One trick we have found that works is to write down all of the negative things that go around in your head about yourself or your trauma. Be honest, get it all down. Now write the name of the person you first heard it from beside each thing. Any surprises? Next, say the things in your head in a funny cartoon voice, like Mickey Mouse or Donald Duck. That helps to break the negative sound track in your head. Try it out now!

If something went wrong that led to your traumatic event, accept the facts of the case. Accept that people make mistakes. Accept the way things are. Accept family and friends who don't understand you, accept your enemies, accept the dead. Accept the past.

A is also for Action. Take Action, move out of yourself, move from the past, move through the grief process, move away from anger, move from the war zone, move forward in life, into the future, get out into the world and make things happen.

Life is a river; it never stays in one place. One thing for sure, sitting on the couch and watching television, or sitting out in the garage and drinking beer, is not going to help you get past your trauma. It numbs things out and makes you feel OK sometimes in the short term, but in the long term it is always going to have negative consequences. Sooner or later, the boozy feeling goes away, or the money runs out, and you are right back where you were before, with your trauma. And now you feel worse, because you start thinking about how this thing has been ruining your life, and how you wish it wouldn't. That's why it's time to take action now, since there never will be a good time to do it. Take action and follow the steps of the START NOW program.

$\underline{A}$ **is also for $\underline{A}$ltruism**, another way to move past yourself. Altruism is the principle or practice of unselfish concern for or devotion to the welfare of others (as opposed to egoism), i.e., when you do something for someone else and expect nothing in return. The fact that *you* are doing it is proof positive that not everyone is out for themselves. This helps you

FIGURE 30: ALTRUISM LEADS TO ACTION AND ACTIVITY

feel less isolated, angry and bitter about the world.

Get involved, become a Big Brother. If you don't see a group that exactly suits you, how about starting your own? Mothers Against Drunk Drivers (MADD) was started by the mothers of (you guessed it) people who were killed by drunk drivers. It used to be that there was little or no enforcement of drunk driving laws; as long as you were able to turn the keys in the ignition of your car you were allowed to roll down the road. Getting caught drunk behind the wheel might get you a fine at best. But the women who organized MADD took action and got legislation passed that toughened the laws against drunk driving and forced the police to take decisive action.

A few years back in Georgia, a psychotic person wandered into a school and hit a little girl in the head with an ax while she was waiting in line for lunch. She survived with injuries. You might think her mother would sink into a well of despondency. But she spurred the State legislators to make laws requiring schools to have appropriate barriers and security so that random people could not wander in and harm the children. She took her grief and anger and turned it to something positive for others. Her altruism not only helped others, it helped her. I think it prevented the development of PTSD.

Research shows that people who transform their trauma into something altruistic do better in the long run than people who isolate and retreat into themselves. This has been found following a range of disasters, from the Columbine school massacre to the Chowchilla bus trauma, where a bunch of children were buried under ground in a school bus.

Granted, you may not be ready to run out and volunteer right after your trauma. You need to follow the initial steps of the START-NOW program first, finding your safety zone and a comfortable and supportive environment in which to start talking about what happened to you.

At some point in your process, it will be good for you, however, to take on altruistic activities. This is more important for traumatized individuals than it is for other people.

Why?

There are a number of reasons. Trauma can have a corrosive effect on our view of ourselves and our environment. The world is a frightening and threatening place. People have dark ulterior motives and cannot be trusted. You may feel like you have no power in the face of your trauma or that your life has no meaning and purpose. You may question the meaning of existence itself or ask out loud to God why this had to happen to you?

By participating in altruistic activities, you meet other good people doing the same thing. These are key people to get in your corner for Seeking Support (see above). By giving of yourself and expecting nothing in return, you help yourself to regain your sense of power and control.

You start to feel like the world has meaning and you have a place in the world and something to give. You have a reason to get up in the morning. You develop a sense of purpose and meaning. People give you positive feedback, which in turn helps your self-esteem and makes you feel better about yourself. Doing something, no matter how small, to prevent the injustice or negative event that happened to you from happening to someone else, can be a powerful thing. Often, people start out focusing on the injustice that affected them, and then go on to become advocates for victims of injustice in general.

R is for <u>Re</u>-Visit the Scene of the Trauma

Take your memories and change them with new facts, insight, wisdom and experience. <u>Re</u>-live your experiences, and then <u>Re</u>-write your story in your own words and on your own terms.

We think all trauma survivors should become writers. We advocate writing a journal about your experiences. Write down what your thoughts and feelings were at the time of the traumatic event. You can use the workbook at the end of this book to help. What happened to you? Write it all down. Just put your pen to paper and keep writing until you feel like you are done. If you need to take a break, do so. You can come back to it later.

What should I write down?

- What were you thinking at the time of the trauma?

- Did you think you were going to die?

- Did you think you had to get someone out of harm's way?

- Were you looking for your attacker?

- Were you thinking that you made a mistake?

- Did someone else screw up?

- Is this is my fault?

- What were you feeling at the time of the trauma?

- Did you feel fear, anger, horror, disgust?

- Did you feel exhilaration?

- Did dangerous events give you an adrenaline rush?

Now is not the time to make judgments about what happened. Just write it exactly how it happened and what was going through your mind. There are no right or wrong answers about this. Just write down whatever you felt. This is for you alone, you don't have to show it to anyone. Only you can say what your feelings are, and there is no such thing as feelings that are "right" or "wrong." You can use the list of emotions at the end of this book to help you identify what your feelings were.

If the memory is in fragments, write the fragments. What you write down may not be factually accurate in terms of "what really happened," but it does represent the facts about how *you* experienced the event. And that is true, even if it is your truth. The fact is that there are multiple perceptions about what happens during a particular event, and no one holds the monopoly on truth, for anything, let alone for a traumatic event.

We used to have a program for veterans with PTSD from the Vietnam War at the West Haven VA Medical Hospital in West Haven, Connecticut, where we would have people write down on piece of paper the names and some characteristics of people who had died in the war that they knew. Then we had a ceremony at a park next to the Long Island Sound near a memorial to veterans of the Vietnam War. We had a funeral pyre and the veterans would read from the paper and then throw it into the pyre.

I will never forget one veteran who read "guy with the purple T-shirt." He could remember hardly anything about this person, and yet his sense of grief and unresolved loss was just as strong twenty years after the war as it was at the time the person died.

R is for Re-visit. It is important to re-visit the scene of your trauma in more ways than one. One way is to write about it or talk about, and re-visit the thoughts, feelings, and physical sensation that occurred at the time.

Another important way is to go back to the place where the event actually happened. You'll be surprised at how different things will be from how you remember it. You may not be ready to go back there right away. Certainly it will fill you with many emotions, including probably fear and distress. Work the earlier parts of your START-

NOW program, seeking safety and support, talking about it, and coming to some acceptance of yourself and the reality of what happened to you, before you take the R step of re-visit.

How We Re-visited Our Own Traumas

Both Lai and I have experienced our own traumas — you are one of the few lucky ones if you've never experienced a traumatic event. Note how each of these two examples involve other people being in danger, not us.

One summer night about ten years ago I stepped out of the front door of our house in Atlanta to walk our dog when I saw something yellow out of the corner of my eye. When I looked more carefully I saw flames coming out of the corner of a house across the street.

I shouted to my wife and then ran back inside to call the fire department. Not getting a signal, I grabbed my shoes and ran out to the backyard to get a better signal on my cell phone and call 911. Then I ran across the street to the house. The entire roof engulfed in flames.

Several people were spraying the house with a garden hose in a feeble attempt to keep the temperature down, but they couldn't get very close to the house because of the heat. I grabbed the hose and tried to advance closer. I could feel the flames licking my face. Smoke billowed from the house. A ground floor window was blown out.

I heard whimpering. Someone was in that room. I tried to push forward, but after a few feet, the heat was too intense. I kept spraying the room with the garden hose and trying to push forward. I screamed at the people behind me to call the Fire Department.

After a few minutes, the whimpering stopped. I turned around. A ring of people stood in the driveway holding hands. The leader, who was the father of the woman who had been in the house and who was unable to escape because she was in a wheelchair, raised the hands of the others and prayed to Jesus. I was in a dream.

The next day, I kept hearing the woman whimpering , playing over and over in my ear, as if I were back in front of the burning house. I had flashes of the flames and the smoke billowing from the house.

Back at my house, late at night after my family had gone to bed, I ventured back across the street. The house had been completely flattened by the fire; only rubble and the vestiges of the walls of what had once been a house remained. I stood where I had been standing with the hose.

I was amazed that the distance between myself and what would have been the window of the room where the poor woman was trapped was less than ten feet. The previous night it seemed like a hundred yards.

I moved back through the former rooms to what had once been the kitchen. I found a broken piece of crockery bowl. I took it home and placed it at the top of a cupboard.

The next day I took out the crockery and examined it. It was darkened by smoke. I wondered about the family who once owned the bowl, and the woman I couldn't save.

The next night I went back to the place where I found the bowl, and stood in the middle of the former kitchen. I let the emotions associated with the disaster, with the family loss, fill me, and I cried.

The next day, I felt better.

Going back to the scene of the disaster helped me, because I created an accurate mental image of the disaster scene that counteracted my traumatic memory of the scene. It turns out that the reality was much different than what I remembered. I believe that over-writing the distorted memory with the realistic memory was beneficial to my approach to the disaster. Also, taking a memento of the event helped me as well.

This next story is from Lai about a traumatic event that happened to her several years ago on the Fourth of July when she witnessed the accidental death of a close friend, and what happened after that.

The last time I saw my friend Ross alive, he stood proudly on the new yacht he and his wife purchased that summer. The tragic events that unfolded on that summer day still remain a mystery to those involved. Not being able to save my friend left me with so many questions and a feeling of guilt that has been a heavy weight. I carry that weight every day...in my body, my thoughts and my heart.

When I found his body on the floor of the boat's cabin, I thought he was still alive. I heard a gurgling noise repeatedly pumping in and out between his lips. A friend, who accompanied us back to the boat, claimed she felt his pulse, so we decided not to administer CPR.

The cabin had a sickening smell, a combination of gasoline and smoke. I along with the other three women on the boat tried to get the windows open, but we failed.

Ross's wife, Christine, was screaming for us to help him. I remember yelling at her to get out of the cabin and go on top of the boat. She was in complete shock.

The three of us used all of our strength to pull him up the steps onto the deck where he could get fresh air. My body became unbelievably fatigued as if I'd just finished running a marathon. We were only able to move him a few inches at a time; he was so heavy. I struggled with my breathing, my strength was depleted and I could barely think straight (I later realized that the cabin was filled with carbon monoxide, which affected my breathing and thinking). I was exhausted. While I held him in my arms as he struggled for air, every muscle in my body was shaking.

When the paramedics arrived at the boat forty-five minutes later, they were not able to revive him. My best friend Kellie drove up to the lake to drive me and my partner to the hospital. As we entered the hospital doors, Christine told us that Ross had died from a heart attack.

The news was difficult to grasp, but I did the best I could to remain calm and carry on. I had to be strong for Christine. She kept repeating, "I can't do this again." Her mother just died three months earlier, so we knew what that meant.

I don't recall talking much about the accident or his death in the immediate aftermath. For the next week, I spent each day preparing for the next. Many friends and family members traveled from out of town for his wake. He was not a religious man; however, his family thought he should be on that last day. I don't remember much of the service, probably due to the drinking and Valium that started first thing that morning. The one thing I do remember was hoping no one would ask about what happened the day he died... and no one did.

As the days and months passed, I found myself trying to keep the thoughts, flashbacks, and moments of sadness from surfacing. I couldn't do much about the nightmares, other than staying up late at night to avoid seeing him in the water, boat or covered on the hospital gurney when I closed my eyes. I distracted myself with going out, meeting new people, drinking, partying, and staying out late. At the time, I felt this was what I needed to do to get over it. The only thing I was doing, though, was destroying the relationship I was involved in and being angry at the world.

As time passed, I was able to convince myself it never happened. I never spoke about it, even with the people who were involved, including my significant other at the time.

Seven months after the accident, I received devastating news. The autopsy report came back: the conclusion was that he actually died from carbon monoxide poisoning. The news forced me to start thinking about it again. All the memories and feelings instantly resurfaced, but this time with more intensity...and with new feelings of extreme guilt. For some reason, believing he died from a heart attack had allowed me to accept his death much more easily.

After learning his death was not from a heart attack, but rather an accident, something within me changed. I felt differently about my experience and about my direct involvement. I started to question all of my decisions and actions, including the possibility that I could have saved his life. Of course, I knew that saving him from a fatal heart attack was next to impossible, even with CPR, but what about leaving him on a boat filled with carbon monoxide? Could any decision that day change his fate of dying from an accident?

Why did I leave the boat? What if I hadn't asked my friends to join me on land? Did I drink way too much? Why couldn't we pull him out of the cabin. Why didn't we administer CPR?

The memories of the events surrounding his death are still very vivid and yet almost surreal. I will always remember the chilling electronic voice from the medical response pack that kept repeating over and over "no pulse, administer CPR." I remember the sirens from the emergency vehicles and the sounds of Christine's screams pleading for us to save his life. I have visions of his dead body on the cabin floor, in the hospital room and lying in the coffin during his wake. I often have nightmares about trying to save an unknown person's life. I find myself running throughout my dreams warning all that someone is going to die but my warnings go unheard, again and again.

After a few years, I realized the trauma of Ross's death had changed me. I thought and felt differently, reacted to the smallest thing, was unable to concentrate on anything for long, and I had less patience. As time went on, I also became less social, had less interest in participating in familiar activities, and stopped making plans for the future...not because I didn't want to be a part of the future, but the future just didn't seem real for me at that time. I can't list all of the ways I overcompensated—and continue to overcompensate—for not saving his life, or how even the smallest trigger catapults me back to the day of his death. I should have done so many things differently that day.

It finally occurred to me at work while I was coming up with the principles to recovering from psychological trauma with Dr. Bremner that I needed to address the trauma in my own life, namely Ross's death. I wanted to feel like my old self again, but to do that I had to go on a journey, a journey to heal from my psychological trauma. I needed to talk about the day Ross died, my feelings about it, re-examine the events of that day, visit the lake where he died, and find friends whom I could trust to share my story and my feelings about what happened. I needed to educate myself about carbon monoxide poisoning, stop the negative thinking and unhealthy behaviors.

And that is exactly what I did.

I applied the steps of the START-NOW program I had helped to develop to my own life. I followed the path of seeking safety and support from friends and people close to me, of sharing my feelings. I went back to the scene of the accident and re-lived it through different eyes.

I bought a boat, which I keep in a marina on the north side of the lake far away from the cove where Ross died, although I have visited the campsite where I grilled hot dogs before Ross died. It looks different; alive with families and laughter. I now have a new memory of the park.

I educated myself about carbon monoxide poisoning. I learned that the blockage of exhaust outlets can cause carbon monoxide to accumulate in the cabin and cockpit area of a boat, and it can only take one or two breaths of it for it to be fatal. I spoke with medical professionals who said that if anyone was able to resuscitate him, which was highly unlikely, he probably would have been left with permanent brain damage, or would remain in a vegetative state. He would not have wanted that. His brain was deprived of oxygen for over forty-five minutes, and I have learned that brain damage has already set in after about eight minutes. These facts helped me realized that I probably could not have saved his life.

Ross's death caused many other past traumas to resurface in my life. For instance, my best friend's boyfriend committed suicide by carbon monoxide poisoning when we were both in high school. My nephews, ages three and five, died when the house I grew up in caught on fire. I started talking about all of those things, mostly with my friend Jennifer, for whose friendship I am very thankful. I also talked with Kellie who has always been there for me. Whenever the topic would surface, she offered a comforting and compassionate look that conveyed "it's OK, you didn't do anything wrong." Her support was so crucial in recovering from the trauma.

I've met several other caring people who encouraged me to talk about the trauma. One of the things I learned is that support from friends, the first step in the START-NOW program, is a crucial part of the recovery process. I have applied the principles of the program to my own life, and I am a firm believer that others can benefit as well.

These stories may not compare to the traumatic events you have lived through. I'm sure most of you have lived through much worse. They are simply examples of how revisiting the event and recreating and rewriting your traumatic event can play a critical role in your recovery process.

I think that my event could have turned into a chronic post-traumatic experience, and to be honest, at the time I was a little afraid of that occurring. I think the key for me was to recognize that this was a traumatic event, and to allow myself to experience my emotions on my own timeline. I didn't try and avoid thinking about it, but as I went through the recovery process there were times when I needed not to think about it and focus on other things. At other times I needed to think about the poor woman trapped in the house and unable to get out because she was in a wheelchair.

I also sought out support from those whom I knew I could rely on: my wife and friends. By watching my own reactions to the event, I gained a better understanding of how the trauma response works. Most importantly, I kept a journal about what had happened, and what my feelings and reactions were. In this way, I was able to re-visit the scene of the event and re-write my own history.

Re-writing My Own Past

Another way to re-create your traumatic events is to literally Re-write a new history about it.

My mother was adopted at birth and never knew who her biological family was. In a way, adoption is like a form of traumatic event, since babies and mothers are separated at birth, sometimes against the wishes of the mother. The circumstances of the adoption are also usually difficult, often involvingck liaison (as was the case with my mother), which fifty years ago was a taboo, or financial circumstances that do not allow the biological parents to raise the child.

When I went back to open her adoption records and find her biological family, I was literally re-writing her family history, and this time with the truth. Not everyone welcomed this new history, but I think finding out the truth had a beneficial mental impact on me.

This story became a book called *The Goose That Laid the Golden Egg* (and no, it is not the children's story). It helped me to write about what happened. You can help yourself, as well, by writing about what happened to you, even if you don't pursue a contract with a publishing company.

Re-writing your history is an essential part of the next step of START-NOW, which is to transform.

T is for Transformation

T is also for Transform. Transform yourself from victim into survivor, from zombie to procreator. Transform yourself through re-writing your history, either literally or figuratively. Transform society to make it a better place. If there are things you don't like about society, or your own life, go do something about it.

Your traumatic event has made you different than other people. That has its good points and its bad points. The bad point is that people don't like people different from them. But the unique aspects of your traumatic experience, the things that only you have experienced, make it possible for you to assume a leadership role. People are always interested in stories where someone underwent a severe challenge and survived or even triumphed. This is the stuff blockbuster movies are made of.

Is there anything you would like to change about the past, the ways things went, make things better? You have the opportunity to become a natural leader, if you want to take it. You can work against the injustices of the world. Your experiences will give you a passion that other people do not have, and that passion will make you more effective than other people.

Most people just float through life, reading the daily paper, going to work, coming home and eating dinner and then watching TV. They've had an un-traumatized life, unlike you, but perhaps they have an uninspired life. Or maybe they were traumatized and retreated into their cocoon.

The only decision you have to make about life is whether you want to take it on:

- What would you like to do with your life?

- What would you like to change?

- What would you like to be when you grow up?

- Is there something related to your trauma that you would like to tackle and change for the better?

There is no better time than now to go out and make a difference in other peoples' lives. And there is no one better to do it than you.

We have gone over the first part of the program, which you have to START. The next question is, when do you do it?

The answer is in the next chapter, which is NOW.

CHAPTER 17: THE TIME TO START IS NOW

In the last chapter we went over the first part of the program, which was

START

S.   is for Safety. Seek Safety and Support.

T.   Talk about your trauma and/or your loss.
Tell people about how you feel.
Translate feelings into words.

A.   is for Action.
Take Action, move beyond your restricted sphere.
It is also for Altruism. Use Altruism as a way to move beyond your trauma.

R.   is for Re-write history.
Re-visit the scene of the trauma.
Re-live it with new eyes.

T.   is for Transform.
Transform yourself from victim into survivor through re-writing your history, and through volunteerism and altruism.
Transform society to make it a better place.

You may ask yourself, when do I START? Can I wait until after I start my new job? After I quit smoking? When I move out of my mother-in-law's house?

The answer is, like quitting smoking or drinking: there never is a good time. The time to START is NOW.

Fortunately, the word NOW spells out the final parts of our program, the part that builds on the parts of the program described in the last chapter.

<u>N</u> is for <u>N</u>otice Other People Around You

<u>N</u>otice other people around you. Notice your world. Go outside of your shell. Reach out to others. Volunteer. Help others.

This is part and parcel of the A is for Altruism part of the program that we outlined in the previous chapter. When people go outside their comfort zone and interact with others, it helps them with their trauma-related symptoms.

Of course, you must master the first part of the program first, i.e., the steps of START having to do with seeking safety and support, including knowing when you need quiet time to yourself, when to construct your boundaries, and when to retreat into one of your safety zones. You may want to review the S. part of the program before you embark on the N. part which involves becoming involved in the world around you.

We recommend to start <u>N</u>oticing others with a therapist. You can use that person as a model and a guide for how you interact with others and relate the story of your trauma. That therapist can in turn guide you on how to branch out and reach out to others.

Another useful forum once you have mastered individual therapy is to try group therapy run by trained mental health professionals. This can be a safe environment to relate the story of your trauma, to learn first-hand how it affects your social interactions with others through the "social laboratory" of the group, and to get honest feedback about how others perceive you as a person and in relationship to your traumatic experiences, and how they have affected your life and your relationships and personality.

Once you have decided that you are ready to Notice the world, you'll find it a life-transforming experience. Trauma survivors have often undergone great trials and have shown incredible resilience in the face of tragedy and loss. The fact that you are reading this book and have gotten this far in your program shows you are a fighter and that you have not given up.

Many people isolate themselves or numb themselves with drugs, alcohol, and other addictions. They may continue to wreak havoc in their personal lives because their internal demons are not under control. You may have gone through a painful divorce or become alienated from your children or from other family and friends. But you are still striving to improve yourself, and for that you can be congratulated. Also, you will have opportunities in the future to make amends, once you have worked on some of the parts of the program in the last chapter that have to do with shoring yourself up in the wake of trauma.

When you are ready to Notice others, reach out to family and friends first. You may need to start with an apology for your behavior. This may or may not be accepted right away. If it is not, don't be discouraged. Just the act of asking for an apology is a start.

While you're at it, don't forget to apologize to yourself if you have been unusually harsh on yourself, or if you have punished yourself through self-destructive behaviors like risky sex, drugs, alcohol, or harming yourself in other ways. Once you have learned to Notice the world, you will be ready to observe yourself and others in a nonjudgmental and loving fashion.

O is for Observe Yourself and Others

Observe yourself and Others. Observe the world around you, and Open yourself to being a part of the world.

This, of course, requires the prior step, which is to Notice Others, but in fact it takes it a step farther. You not only Notice others, but you Observe them in a non-partial, nonjudgmental way.

A lot of people with difficult childhoods or who came from an environment where they were subjected to trauma, have had to deal with harsh and critical people. Sometimes these people get incorporated into our heads like a soundtrack, even people whom we don't like or that we know were cruel and emotionally abusive (as well as possibly being sexually and/or emotionally abusive) people.

Our research shows that people who are victims of sexual and/or physical abuse are almost ALWAYS also subject to emotional abuse. This involves persistent and negative comments — the effects of this can be especially detrimental when delivered to young children. Take a look at some of the questions from the Early Trauma Inventory, which we developed and which is available on our website for free, and see if any of the emotional abuse questions apply to you. This inventory is also in the workbook below.

Before the age of 18, did any of these things ever happen to you?

Physical Abuse
1. Were you ever slapped in the face with an open hand?
2. Were you ever burned with hot water, a cigarette or something else?
3. Were you ever punched or kicked?
4. Were you ever hit with an object that was thrown at you?
5. Were you ever pushed or shoved?

Emotional Abuse
1. Were you often put down or ridiculed?
2. Were you often ignored or made to feel that you didn't count?
3. Were you often told you were no good?
4. Most of the time were you treated in a cold, uncaring way or
5. Did your parents or caretakers often fail to understand you or your needs?

Sexual Abuse
1. Were you ever touched in an intimate or private part of your body (e.g. breast, thighs, genitals) in a way that surprised you or made you feel uncomfortable?
2. Did you ever experience someone rubbing their genitals against you?
3. Were you ever forced or coerced to touch another person in an intimate or private part of their body?
4. Did anyone ever have genital sex with you against your will?
5. Were you ever forced or coerced to perform oral sex on someone against your will?

Did you answer "yes" to three or more of the emotional abuse questions? If so, then you were emotionally abused as a child. Who did it to you? Your parents? Step parent? Siblings? Kids at school?

There's a good chance it could be all of the above. We know the effects of emotional abuse are particularly corrosive and can persist for years, even if we don't want it to or tell ourselves to "just get over it."

You should have learned through this book by now that this is not the answer.

So what is the answer?

You will need to start by observing yourself and others uncritically and objectively:

- Are you quick to judge others?

- Are you harsh and unfair?

- Do you ever catch yourself acting in ways like the behaviors of the parent/step parent/mean uncle you can't stand? The one you swore you would grow up and never be like? The difference between you and that person is that you are actively trying to do something about yourself, unlike the other person who either went to his or her grave unchanged or is continuing to act the same way. Maybe they are drunk right now or carrying on in their fifth abusive marriage. Maybe you have no idea what they are doing because you cut off contact with them years ago although their negative soundtrack plays on in your head.

- What is the content of your negative soundtrack? Does it say that you are no good, that you will never amount to anything? Does it say that you are too isolated, too flirtatious, too self-centered, too chatty?

We recommend writing down on a list of all the people who said negative things and under each person make a list of the negative comments they made about you. You can use the workbook at the end of this book.

Now make a list of the negative comments about yourself that play in your mind. Be honest. Write down to each comment the person who said it. Our guess is that some people will pop up again and again. Think about the basis of the authority of that person's opinion. Were they a loving, selfless, giving person, free from alcohol and drugs or other addictions, who maintained positive long term relationships with others?

Yeah, we didn't think so. There's a good chance that you don't even know where they are, or maybe they're dead.

Are you going to let this person control the soundtrack of your brain? Probably not a good idea. But the first step is to recognize the soundtrack for what it is. You might never have thought about it before.

One trick we've found helpful for dealing with it is to force yourself to recite the soundtrack, but do it in the voice of a funny cartoon character, like Mickey Mouse. Try it out and see what you think. Next time the soundtrack sneaks up on you, don't try and fight it, but just let it come out using that funny voice.

No matter an individual's personality, you can always find something to criticize. You can break the chain by starting right now to observe your mental reactions and the behaviors of others nonjudgmentally, and identify what they are and what their triggers are. Once you think nonjudgmentally you actually start to develop more control, because then you are no longer slave to your judgments and automatic thinking. Get it?

Once you have passed that step, you will start to see the world for the wonderful place it can potentially be. Which brings us to our final step of the program.

<u>W</u> is for <u>W</u>onder about the World

<u>W</u> is for <u>W</u>onder about the <u>W</u>orld: see things through new eyes. <u>W</u>in your fight against traumatic stress. If we let it be, the World can be a Wonderful place.

Take a step outside. Is it a sunny day? Are the birds chirping? Take a look at the trees, the sky. Isn't it beautiful? Or if it is raining, bring your umbrella and take a walk. Rain has a beauty of its own.

How are things going for you? Are you starting to feel better about yourself and others? Do you see some ray of hope at the end of the tunnel? Are you getting along a little better with your family and friends? Do you see anything about your life journey, including the traumatic part, that gives you a sense of meaning, or a feeling of mission about making the world a better place? If you have read this far, our guess is that on some level you do. So hats off to you.

CHAPTER 18: THE START-NOW IN REVIEW: LET'S GET STARTED!

Now let's review the material of this chapter and the previous one, and see where we are and where we may need to go. We have the START-NOW program.

START NOW

S. is for Safety. Seek Safety and Support. Sometimes Silence is nice.

T. Talk about your trauma and/or your loss. Tell people about how you feel. Translate feelings into words.

A. is for Acceptance. Accept what happened to you. Accept yourself. Accept the past. It is also for Action. Take Action, move beyond your restricted sphere. Move out into the world and forward into the future. A is also for Altruism, or doing things for others. Altruism is a way of moving beyond yourself. When you practice Altruism and help others, you are really helping yourself. Use Altruism as a way to move beyond your trauma.

R. is for Re-write history. Re-visit the scene of the trauma. Re-live it with new eyes. Take your memories and Re-visit them with new wisdom, knowledge, and experience.

T. is for Transform. Transform yourself from victim into survivor through re writing your history, and through volunteerism and altruism. Transform society to make it a better place.

N. is for Notice other people around you. Go outside of your shell. Reach out to others. Volunteer. Help others.

O. is for Observe and yourself and Others. Observe the world around you, and Open yourself to being a part of **the world.**

W. is for Wonder about the World. See things through new eyes. Win your fight against traumatic stress.

You probably won't progress through the START-NOW program in a logical and seamless way, nor do we expect you to, but you'll need the lessons of the earlier parts of the program in order to tackle the later parts.

Don't rush it. There is nothing worse than force feeding yourself or faking it. Some parts of the program may be more helpful than others. Not everyone is the same.

You may have to go back over earlier parts of the program after you have already moved forward. You should think about it like peeling an onion rather than going on a journey that advances from one rail station to the next with no opportunity to go back.

That may mean re-reading this book several times, as well as other books about the trauma recovery process, to help you gain insights.

The next step is to start working your program by filling out the work book at the end of this book, if you haven't started to do so already.

One thing we are sure about, it is never too late to START-NOW!

The START NOW Program of Self Healing: Self-heal Manual

Let's get STARTed!

S. is for Safety. Seek Safety and Support. Sometimes Silence is nice.

T. Talk about your trauma and/or your loss. Tell people close to you about how you feel. Translate feelings into words.

A. is for Acceptance. Accept what happened to you. What happened was not right, was not ideal, maybe it was unlucky. But nothing you can do now will change it. Accept yourself. Accept the past.
A is also for Action. Take Action, move beyond your restricted sphere. Move out into the world and forward into the future. A is also for Altruism, or doing things for others. Altruism is a way of moving beyond yourself. When you practice Altruism and help others, you are really helping yourself. Use Altruism as a way to move beyond your trauma.

R. is for Re-write history. Re-visit the scene of the trauma.Re-live it with new eyes. Take your memories and change them with new facts, insight, wisdom, knowledge, and experience.

T. is for Transform. Transform yourself from victim into survivor through re writing your history, and through volunteerism and altruism. Transform society to make it a better place. If there are things you don't like about society, or your own life, change it.

N. is for Notice other people around you. Go outside of your shell. Reach out to others. Volunteer. Help others.

O. is for Observe and yourself and Others. Observe the world around you, and Open yourself to being a part of **the world.**

W. is for Wonder about the World. See things through new eyes. Win your fight against traumatic stress.

Now we're going to start putting some of the things we have learned into action. That starts with re-visiting our traumas and re-writing the history. To do that we're going to do some of the journaling exercises we talked about before. By now you should have already covered some of the points of the START NOW Program that have allowed you to get this far, like Seeking Safety and Support. Or maybe you needed some time for Silence. If you need to, go back and re-visit those points now. If you get overwhelmed or flooded while doing these exercises, step back and take it easy. Give yourself some time, and don't get down on yourself because you "failed." Remember, this is a circular process. You can come back around to it again after you have reviewed the earlier points again. Congratulate yourself on getting this far! Most people don't even try to make the journal.

Answer the questions below by writing them down. Or maybe you want to write a poem, write a song, or make a painting. Let's get started!

Who is in your family? (list wife, kids, parents, brothers, sisters, close relatives)

Name	Relationship to you

Were you separated from family? How did this go? How has it been since you came back?

_____
_____
_____
_____
_____
_____

_____
_____
_____
_____
_____

_____

Your support group is the people you can count on, can talk to. This could include your wife, husband, girlfriend, boyfriend, significant other, brother, sister, brother, father, mother, or your friend or someone at work. Make a list of the people in your support group below. They don't have to be your best friend. And if you don't want to name them (or your relationship to you), put an X, or make something up. Rate how supportive each person is, from 1 (least supportive) to 10 (most supportive).

Name	Relationship to you	Rating

Now write something about those some of the people, why or why not they are supportive. How you do (or do not) seek support from them? What you do together? How have they (or have not) helped you?

_____
_____
_____
_____
_____
_____
_____
_____
_____
_____
_____
_____
_____
_____

Name five physical places that make you feel safe (e.g, your home or a room in your home, a lake, some place in the mountains, a favorite childhood place or hideaway, etc.).

_____
_____
_____
_____
_____
_____
_____
_____
_____
_____
_____
_____

Now write about times you thought about those places, how it made you feel (e.g., thinking about something good, or a good memory of a place or a person, when things were going bad). Or maybe times you actually went there to feel better.

_____

_____

_____

_____

_____

_____

_____

_____

_____

_____

_____

_____

_____

_____

Name five mental places you can go to feel safe (e.g., thinking about my kids, imagining a scene on the beach or in the mountains).

_____

_____

_____

_____

_____

_____

_____

_____

_____

_____

_____

_____

_____

Now write about times you went to those mental places and how you used them (e.g., thinking about something good, or a good memory of a place or a person, when things were going bad).

_____

_____

_____

_____

_____
_____
_____
_____
_____
_____
_____
_____

Now write about a frightening or negative thing that happened to you (e.g. being physically injured, being molested or sexually assaulted, seeing someone else seriously injured or killed, getting in a car accident, not being able to help or prevent a situation like a death or injury, etc.). Describe it in as much detail as possible.

_____
_____
_____
_____
_____
_____
_____
_____
_____
_____

What were you thinking at the time (e.g., I'm going to get killed, I've got to get someone else out of harm's way, someone screwed up, this is my fault...)?

_____
_____
_____
_____
_____

_____

_____

_____

_____

_____

_____

_____

What were you feeling at the time (fear, rush, anger, horror, disgust, exhilaration)? Use the list of emotion words at the end of the manual or in Appendix A.

_____

_____

_____

_____

_____

_____

_____

_____

_____

_____

_____

_____

What were you seeing at the time? What memory flashes back the most? What were you hearing? Was there anything touching you or injuring you? Were there any smells?

_____

_____

_____

_____

_____

_____

_____

_____

_____

_____

_____

Now write about a second memory of a frightening or negative thing that happened to you (e.g. physically injured, being molested or sexually assaulted, got in a car accident, seeing others killed or wounded, not being able to help or prevent a situation, etc.). Describe it in as much detail as possible.

_____
_____
_____
_____
_____
_____
_____
_____
_____
_____
_____
_____

What were you seeing at the time? What memory flashes back the most? What were you hearing? Was there anything touching you or injuring you? Were there any smells?

_____
_____
_____
_____
_____
_____
_____
_____
_____
_____
_____
_____

What were you feeling at the time (fear, rush, anger, horror, disgust, exhilaration, use the list of emotion words)?

_____

_____

_____

_____

_____

_____

_____

_____

_____

_____

_____

Now write about a third memory of a frightening or negative thing that happened to you (e.g. physically injured, being molested or sexually assaulted, got in a car accident, seeing others killed or wounded, not being able to help or prevent a situation, etc.). Describe it in as much detail as possible.

_____

_____

_____

_____

_____

_____

_____

_____

_____

_____

_____

What were you seeing at the time? What memory flashes back the most? What were you hearing? Was there anything touching you or injuring you? Were there any smells?

_____
_____
_____
_____
_____
_____
_____
_____
_____
_____
_____
_____
_____

What were you feeling at the time (fear, rush, anger, horror, disgust, exhilaration, use the list of emotion words)?

_____
_____
_____
_____
_____
_____
_____
_____
_____
_____
_____
_____

Is there anything about any of these memories that you have trouble accepting? (e.g. people were killed that didn't have to be, we shouldn't have been there, mistakes I made, what would have happened if a different decision was made, could I have prevented it, could I have helped?) Write about those.

_____
_____
_____
_____

_____

_____

_____

_____

_____

_____

_____

_____

Is there anything you would like to change about the past, the ways things went, make things better? Write about that.

_____

_____

_____

_____

_____

_____

_____

_____

_____

_____

Is there anything you would like to change about the future, make things better? Write about that.

_____

_____

_____

_____

_____

_____

_____

_____

_____

Make a list of all the negative comments you heard as a child from
your parent/step parent/uncle/sibling/schoolmates. First write
down the person, then make a list of comments. Make a different list
for each person.

_____

_____

_____

_____

_____

_____

_____

_____

_____

_____

_____

_____

ABOUT THE AUTHORS

J. Douglas Bremner, M.D.

J. Douglas Bremner, M.D. is Professor of Psychiatry and Radiology and Director of the Emory Clinical Neuroscience Research Unit (ECNRU) at Emory University School of Medicine and the Atlanta VA Medical Center in Atlanta, Georgia. He spends one day a week seeing soldiers returning from Iraq and Afghanistan and performing assessments on other veterans with mental health complaints.

He has a long history of experience in the field of PTSD and trauma dating back to his role as the Medical Director of the first inpatient unit for PTSD at the National Center for PTSD in West Haven, Connecticut. His research on changes in the brain and symptoms of trauma, dissociation, and PTSD are amongst the most highly cited in his field.

He is the author of several best-selling books including Does Stress Damage the Brain? and Before You Take That Pill as well as the personal narrative The Goose that Laid the Golden Egg.

The current book represents his effort to give back his knowledge and experience to trauma sufferers. He hopes it will provide a resource that lets sufferers help themselves to heal and recover…and that doesn't cost too much.

Dr. Bremner lives in Atlanta, Georgia, with his wife. He has a teenage son who is currently an exchange student in Trentino-Alto

Adige, Italy, and a daughter who is a senior at the University of Chicago.

Lai Reed, M.B.A

Lai Reed, M.B.A., is Associate Director of the Emory Clinical Neuroscience Research Unit at Emory University School of Medicine in Atlanta, Georgia. She has worked for over a decade on clinical research studies of both victims of childhood abuse and combat veterans with PTSD.

Prior to that she ran an inpatient treatment unit for the treatment of children and adolescents with a history of childhood trauma - substance abuse disorders and was Director of an emergency shelter for children.

She currently lives in Decatur, Georgia.

APPENDIX A: EMOTIONAL WORDS

Afraid	Alive	Angry	Apprehensive
Ashamed	Awkward	Bitter	Brave
Calm	Capable	Competent	Concerned
Confused	Contemptuous	Courageous	Defeated
Dejected	Dependent	Depressed	Despairing
Desperate	Devastated	Disappointed	Discouraged
Disgusted	Distrustful	Embarrassed	Exasperated
Fearful	Foolish	Forgiving	Frantic
Frustrated	Furious	Guilty	Hateful
Helpless	Hopeless	Horrified	Hostile
Humiliated	Hurt	Ignored	Impatient
Inadequate	Incompetent	Indecisive	Inferior
Inhibited	Insecure	Irritated	Isolated
Jealous	Lonely	Melancholy	Miserable
Misunderstood	Muddled	Needy	Neglected
Old	Outraged	Overwhelmed	Panicky
Peaceful	Pessimistic	Phony	Preoccupied
Pressured	Provoked	Quiet	Relaxed
Relieved	Regretful	Rejected	Resentful
Revengeful	Sad	Self-conscious	Self-reliant
Shy	Sorry	Strong	Stubborn
Stupid	Terrified	Threatened	Tired
Touchy	Trapped	Troubled	Unappreciated
Unattractive	Uncertain	Uncomfortable	Uneasy
Unfulfilled	Used	Uptight	Victimized
Violated	Vulnerable	Weary	Wishy-washy
Worn-out	Worried		

APPENDIX B: RESOURCES FOR TRAUMA VICTIMS

National Center for Victims of Crime. 1-800-FYI-CALL. This is a comprehensive database of more than 6,700 community service agencies throughout the country that directly support victims of crime.

Trauma Treatment. If you are a veteran, look under Health Benefits and Services at www.va.gov. If you are not, look in the "County Government Offices" section of your phone book under your county and look for "Health Services" and "Mental Health.". If you have insurance, ask your doctor. If you think you may have a psychiatric disorder and know what it is based on what you have learned from this book, let him know. He can't read your mind and know what you need.

Anxiety Disorders of America (ADAA). The ADAA has a referral network of therapists including a list of PTSD experts, as well as a self help network. I am on the Scientific Advisory Board and personally approve their recommendations for self-help books, so go to their on-line book store for your self-help book selections. I think it is a good idea to buy self-help books and try to follow them. www.adaa.org.

The *National Institute of Mental Health (NIMH)* is a great resource for information. It is run by a friend of mine who came from Emory, and the Mood and Anxiety Disorders Program is run by my ex-boss, with whom I did the research described in this book, and who knows a lot about trauma. www.nih.gov.

The *National Center for PTSD* is where I spent the first part of my career treating patients and doing research in PTSD. Their web site has some great information. Research articles are also included, if you want to read them, you can download them. ncptsd.org

Sidran Press is a great place for books about trauma. They also have a list of professional referrals. www.sidran.org

David Baldwin has a great web page that has a wealth of information about trauma, resources, information and treatment. He is a clinical psychologist in Eugene, Oregon. www.trauma-pages.com

If you have been abused or know of someone who has been abused, you should contact your local *Department of Child and Family Services.* Reporting of abuse is required by the law.

The Oldways Preservation and Exchange Trust is a nonprofit foundation dedicated to promotion of the Mediterranean Diet and other healthy behaviors. http://oldwayspt.org

National Domestic Abuse Hotline: 1–800–799–SAFE(7233) or TTY 1-800-787-3224.

National Child Abuse Hotline: 1-800-4-A-CHILD (1-800-422-4453)

Eldercare Help Locator (not 24 hours) 1-800-677-1116

APPENDIX C: LIST OF IMAGES AND DIAGRAMS

(permissions, sources and credits)

Figure 1.   Hippocampal volume in PTSD, page 26

From figure 4.2 in *Does Stress Damage the Brain? Understanding Trauma-related Disorders from a Mind-Body Perspective*, by J. Douglas Bremner. Copyright © 2002 by J. Douglas Bremner, M.D. Used by permission of W. W. Norton & Company, Inc.

Figure 2.   Diagram of Human Brain, page 34

Modified from figure in Wikipedia derived from *Gray's Anatomy*.

Figure 3.   Lobes of the Cerebrum, page 36

Modified from figure in Wikipedia derived from *Gray's Anatomy*.

Figure 4.   Human body and glands, page 41

From figure 3.3 in *Does Stress Damage the Brain? Understanding Trauma-related Disorders from a Mind-Body Perspective*, by J. Douglas Bremner. Copyright © 2002 by J. Douglas Bremner, M.D. Used by permission of W. W. Norton & Company, Inc.

Figure 5.   Diagram of a human neuron, page 43

Used with permission of Hollowtree Workshops © 2014

Figure 6.   Brain activation with exposure to traumatic reminders, page 52

From figure 4.5 in *Does Stress Damage the Brain? Understanding Trauma-related Disorders from a Mind-Body Perspective*, by J. Douglas Bremner. Copyright © 2002 by J. Douglas Bremner, M.D. Used by permission of W. W. Norton & Company, Inc.

Figure 7.   Need to Escape, page 56

By Igor Petrov via license from Shutterstock.

Figure 8.   Trauma Spectrum Disorders, page 67

Adapted from *Does Stress Damage the Brain? Understanding Trauma-related Disorders from a Mind-Body Perspective*, by J. Douglas Bremner. Copyright © 2002 by J. Douglas Bremner, M.D. Used by permission of W. W. Norton & Company, Inc.

Figure 9.   DSM-IV-TR Criteria for Major Depression, page 69

© 2014 J. Douglas Bremner, adapted from DSM-IV-TR APA. (2000). *DSM-IV-TR: Diagnostic and Statistical Manual of Mental Disorders*. Washington, D.C.: American Psychiatric Press.

Figure 10.   DSM-IV-TR Criteria for Post Traumatic Stress Disorder (PTSD), page 75

Adapted from DSM-IV-TR APA. (2000). *DSM-IV-TR: Diagnostic and Statistical Manual of Mental Disorders*. Washington, D.C.: American Psychiatric Press.

Figure 11.   Stages of Grief, page 120

By Marekulasz via license from Shutterstock

Figure 12.   Antidepressant Medications – Uses and Risks, page 137

From BEFORE YOU TAKE THAT PILL, by J. Douglas Bremner, © 2008 J. Douglas Bremner, used by permission of Avery Publishing, an imprint of the Penguin Group.

Figure 13.   Antipsychotic Medications: Uses and Risks, page 147

From BEFORE YOU TAKE THAT PILL, by J. Douglas Bremner, © 2008 J. Douglas Bremner, used by permission of Avery Publishing, an imprint of the Penguin Group. Public domain.

Figure 14. Insomnia Medications: Uses and Risks, page 153

From BEFORE YOU TAKE THAT PILL, by J. Douglas Bremner, © 2008 J. Douglas Bremner, used by permission of Avery Publishing, an imprint of the Penguin Group.

Figure 15. Sources of Stress, page 170

By squarelogo via license from Shutterstock

Figure 16. Mediterranean Diet food pyramid, page 183

Used with permission of Oldways Preservation and Exchange Trust. http://oldwayspt.org. Copyright © 2012 Oldways Preserva-tion and Exchange Trust.

Figure 17. Symptoms of Alcohol & Substance Abuse, page 185

© 2014 J. Douglas Bremner, adapted from DSM-IV-TR APA. (2000). *DSM-IV-TR: Diagnostic and Statistical Manual of Mental Disorders.* Washington, D.C.: American Psychiatric Press.

Figure 18. Building Relationships, page 189

By Otmar Winterleitner via license from Dreamstime

Figure 19. Changing Your Conversations, page 197

Adapted from: Wachs, Kim M. *Relationships for Dummies.* Wiley, 2002.

Figure 20. Combat Deployment Can Cause Problems, page 202

By John Gomez via Shutterstock

Figure 21. Increasing suicide rates in veterans of Iraq andAfghanistan, page 141

Figure from thinkprogress.org, source of information Department of Defence. Copyright © 2012 Center for American Progress Action Fund (CAPAF). Accessed 8/10/13 from http://thinkprogress.org/security/2012/06/08/496604/military-suicide/

Figure 22.   The Soldier Returns Home, page 207

By bikeriderlondon via Shutterstock

Figure 23.   Callaway Homecoming Initiative brochure, page 210

Copyright © 2012 Callaway Gardens, used by permission of Callaway Gardens.

Figure 24.   Women are Soldiers, too, page 214

By John Gomez via Shutterstock

Figure 25.   Neural Activity in the Fight or Flight Response, page 216

Used with permission of Hollowtree Workshops © 2014

Figure 26.   The Physiology of Fight-or-Flight Reactions, page 218

By Sebastian Kaulitzki via Shutterstock.

Figure 27.   Start the START-NOW Program, page 228

By Woodooart via Dreamstime.

Figure 28.   Talking and Telling, page 236

By Nyul via Dreamstime.

Figure 29.   Accept What Happened, page 239

By Aydindurdu via Dreamstime.

Figure 30.   Altruism Helps, page 242

By Lucian Milasan via Dreamstime.

APPENDIX D: BIBLIOGRAPHY AND RECOMMENDED READING

American Psychiatric Association. *DSM-IV-TR: Diagnostic and Statistical Manual of Mental Disorders.* American Psychiatric Press, Washington, D.C. 2000.

Bremner, J.D., Southwick, S.M., Brett, E., Fontana, A., Rosenheck, A., Charney, D.S. Dissociation and posttraumatic stress disorder in Vietnam combat veterans. *American Journal of Psychiatry.* 1992; 149:328-332.

Bremner, J.D., Southwick, S.M., Johnson, D.R., Yehuda, R., Charney, D.S. Childhood physical abuse and combat-related posttraumatic stress disorder in Vietnam veterans. *American Journal of Psychiatry.* 1993; 150:235-239.

Bremner, J. D., Southwick, S.M., Darnell, A., Charney, D.S. Chronic PTSD in Vietnam combat veterans: Course of illness and substance abuse. *American Journal of Psychiatry.* 1996; 153:369-375.

Bremner, J.D., Vermetten, E., & Mazure, C.M. Development and preliminary psychometric properties of an instrument for the measurement of childhood trauma: The Early Trauma Inventory. *Depression and Anxiety.* 2000; 12:1-12.

Bremner, J. Douglas. *Does Stress Damage the Brain? Understanding Trauma-related Disorders from a Mind-Body Perspective.* WW Norton, New York, NY, 2002.

Bremner, J. Douglas. *Brain Imaging Handbook.* WW Norton, New York, NY, 2005.

Bremner, J. Douglas. *Before You Take that Pill: Why the Drug Industry May Be Bad For Your Health: Risks and Side Effects You Won't Find on the Label of Commonly Prescribed Drugs and Supplements.* Avery/Penguin, New York, NY, 2008.

Bremner, J. Douglas. Combat-related Psychiatric Syndromes. In: *Functional Pain Syndromes: Presentation and Pathophysiology.* Mayer,

Emeran A., and Bushnell M.C. (Eds.); Seattle, WA, US: IASP Press, 2009. pp. 169-183.

Bremner, Doug. *The Goose That Laid the Golden Egg – Accutane, the truth that had to be told.* Right Publishing, San Francisco, CA, 2011.

Bremner, Doug. *The Fastest Growing Religion on Earth: How Genealogy Captured the Brains and Imaginations of Americans.* Laughing Cow Books, Atlanta, GA, 2013.

Bremner, J. Douglas. Emory Clinical Neuroscience Research Unit (ECNRU) web site, http://www.psychiatry.emory.edu/research/laboratories/bremner/index.html accessed September 14, 2014.

Briere, John. *Child Abuse Trauma: Theory and Treatment of the Lasting Effects.* Sage Publications, Newbury Park, CA, 1992.

Brondolo, Elizabeth, and Xavier Amador. *Break the Bipolar Cycle: A Day-by-Day Guide to Living with Bipolar Disorder.* McGraw-Hill Books, New York, 2008.

Brown, Nina W. *Children of the Self-Absorbed: A Grown Up's Guide to Getting Over Narcissistic Parents. 2* nd *Edition.* New Harbinger Publications, Oakland, CA, 2008.

Cyrulnik, Boris. *The Whispering of Ghosts: Trauma and Resilience.* Other Press, New York, 2005.

Donaldson-Pressman, Stephanie, and Robert M. Pressman. *The Narcissistic Family: Diagnosis and Treatment.* Josey-Bass, New York, 1997.

Freud, Anna. *Ego and the Mechanisms of Defense.* International Universities Press, New York, 1965.

Freud, Sigmund. *Introductory Lectures on Psychoanalysis.* WW Norton, New York, 1965.

Freud, Sigmund. *The Interpretation of Dreams.* Avon, New York, 1965.

Freyd, Jennifer J. *Betrayal Trauma: The logic of forgetting childhood abuse.* Harvard Press, Cambridge, Mass., 1996.

Gabriel, Richard A. *No More Heroes: Madness and Psychiatry in War.* Hill and Wang, New York, 1987.

Herman, Judith. *Trauma and Recovery: The aftermath of violence – from domestic abuse to political terror.* Basic Books, New York, 1997.

Jung, Carl G. *Man and His Symbols.* Dell Nonfiction, New York, 1964.

Kabat-Zinn, Jon. *Full Catastrophic Living: Using the Wisdom of your Body and Mind to Face Stress, Pain, and Illness.* Delta Health Psychology, New York, 1990.

Kessler, R.C., Sonnega, A., Bromet, E., Hughes, M., Nelson, C.B. Posttraumatic stress disorder in the national comorbidity survey. *Archives of General Psychiatry.* 1995;52:1048-1060.

Kessler, R.C., Berglund, P., Demler, O., Jin, R., Koretz, D., Merikangas, K.R., Rush, A.J., Walters, E.E., Wang, P.S. The epidemiology of major depressive disorder: Results from the national comorbidity survey replication (ncs-r). *JAMA.* 2003;289:3095-3105

Kirmayer, L. J., Lemelson, R., & Barad, M. (Eds.). *Understanding Trauma: Integrating Biological, Clinical and Cultural Perspectives.* Cambridge University Press, Cambridge, United Kingdom, 2007.

Kubler-Ross, Elisabeth. *On Death and Dying.* Scribner, New York, 1969.

Langs, Robert. *Rating Your Psychotherapist: Find out whether your therapy is working — and what to do if it's not.* Henry Holt, New York, 1989.

LeDoux, Joseph. *The Emotional Brain: The mysterious underpinnings of emotional life.* Simon & Schuster, New York, 1996.

Levine, Peter A. *Waking the Tiger: Healing Trauma.* North Atlantic Books, Berkeley, CA, 1997.

Mehl-Madrona, Lewis. *Healing the Mind through the Power of Story: The Promise of Narrative Psychiatry.* Bear & Company, Rochester, VT, 2010.

Middelton-Moz, Jane. *Shame and Guilt: Masters of Disguise.* Health Communications, Inc., Deerfield Beach, FL, 1990.

Miller, Alice. *The Drama of the Gifted Child: How Narcissistic Parents Form and Deform the Emotional Lives of Their Talented Children.* Basic Book, New York, 1981.

Miller, Alice. *Prisoners of Chilhood: The Drama of the Gifted Child and the Search for the True Self.* Basic Book, New York, 1987.

Ross, Colin. *Dissociative Identity Disorder: Diagnosis, Clinical Features, and Treatment of Multiple Personality.* Wiley Press, New York, 1996

Ross, Colin. *The Great Psychiatry Scam: One Shrink's Personal Journey.* Manitou Press, Richardson, Texas, 2008.

Ross, Colin and Naomi Halpern. *Trauma Model Therapy: A treatment approach for trauma, dissociation and complex comorbidity.* Manitou Communications, Richardson, Texas, 1989.

Ross, Colin. *The Trauma Model: A Solution to the Problem of Comorbidity in Psychiatry.* Manitou Press, Richardson, Texas, 2000.

Saigh, Phillip; Bremner, J. Douglas (Editors): *Posttraumatic Stress Disorder: A Comprehensive Text.* Allyn & Bacon, Needham Heights, MA, 1999.

Schlesinger, Laura: *Cope with it!* Kensington Press, New York, 2000.

Shay, Jonathan. *Achilles and Vietnam: Combat Trauma and the Undoing of Character.* Simon & Schuster, New York, 1995.

Siegel, Daniel J. *The Developing Mind: Toward a Neurobiology of Interpersonal Experience.* Guilford Press, New York, 1999.

Stewart, W.F., Ricci, J.A., Chee, E., Hahn, S.R., Morganstein, D. Cost of lost productive work time among us workers with depression. *JAMA.* 2003;289:3135-3144.

Terr, Lenore: *Too Scared to Cry: How Trauma Affects Children… and Ultimately Us All.* Basic Books, New York, 1990.

Vaccarino, Viola, and Bremner, J. Douglas. Cardiovascular disease and depression. In: *Braunwald's Heart Disease,* 2011.

van der Kolk, Bessel. *Psychological Trauma.* APA Press, Washington DC, 1987.

van der Kolk, Bessel. *The Body Keeps the Score: Brain, Mind and Body in the Healing of Psychological Trauma.* Viking Adult, 2014.

Wachs, Kim M. *Relationships for Dummies.* Wiley, 2002.

Whitfield, Charles L. *A Gift to Myself: A Personal Workbook and Guide to the Bestselling 'Healing the Child Within'.* Health Communications Inc., Deerfield Beach, FL, 1987.

Whitfield, Charles L. *Healing the Child Within.* Health Communications Inc., Deerfield Beach, FL, 1987.

Whitfield, Charles L. *The Truth About Mental Illness.* Health Communications Inc., Deerfield Beach, FL, 2004.

Whitmore-Hickman, Martha. *Healing After Loss: Daily Meditations for Recovery from Grief.*

Winnicott, Donald. *The Family and Individual Development.* Tavistock Press, Tavistock, Mass., 1965.

Wolfe, Thomas. *You Can't Go Home Again.* Scribner, New York, 2011.

INDEX

Made in the USA
Charleston, SC
02 May 2015